"If the Kingdom of Heaven is like a treasure hidden in a field, *Whispers of Rest* is a map to that peace uninhibited."

Rebecca Marie Jo, Managing Editor at
RELEVANT Magazine

"In a culture where we wear busyness like a status symbol, slowing down and resting can feel uncomfortable, like failure. In reality, we're wearing ourselves out, inviting anxiety and restlessness in. *Whispers of Rest* calls us to a counter-cultural way of understanding rest—as something deeply good and deeply essential to our flourishing."

Kelly Givens, Senior Editor of iBelieve.com

"Bonnie inspires us to spark joy, experience God's peace and celebrate the beloved that we already are. This intimate book of rest will bring you to Jesus in fresh and meaningful ways."

Rebekah Lyons, author of *You Are Free* and
Founder of Q Women

"Bonnie has bravely journeyed and shares her insights with us so we can learn alongside. She has spoken words of encouragement to me that have changed how I love my husband, children and friends and the way I live every day. Her heart is true and beautiful. This book will change lives."

Lisa Leonard, Founder, Creative Director
lisaleonard.com

"Bonnie has a gift of pointing out a path of small steps that lead to big love from our Creator. This book is a trail guide to help us move toward the love Christ already has for us—and has had for us since time began—and invites us to enjoy simple

practices that are soaked in truth. I'm grateful she's sharing her gift with all of us in this book."

Tsh Oxenreider, author of At Home in the World and
Founder TheArtofSimple.net

"The thing I love most about Bonnie Gray is that she lives every word she writes. Bonnie boldly goes first, so she can guide the rest of us into sacred spaces of rest along paths she has already taken. A 40-day journey with this book with lead you through soulful and scriptural practices that remind you what it feels like to be God's beloved, and will stir things in your soul that have laid dormant, waiting for the right time to come back to life. Reading this book will help you feel like you can breathe again."

Mandy Arioto, President and CEO
MOPS International

"Although we live on opposite sides of the continent, Bonnie and I have walked the same journey of finding peace with Jesus, even through anxiety. In Whispers of Rest, Bonnie does a masterful job of guiding readers to the quiet corners of our hearts, where we can hear the still, small voice of our Father reminding us that we are His beloved. A welcome reminder to distance ourselves from the cacophony of our daily lives, Whispers of Rest is like a 'reset' button for a worried, hurried heart."

Josh Wilson, award-winning Songwriter/Recording
Artist, This Was Then, This Is Now

"With soul-stirring insights, thought-provoking reflections and biblical encouragement, Bonnie Gray helps us see our deep need for spiritual rest and offers practical ways to find it in the midst of our everyday lives. Whispers of Rest created a place for my heart to breathe and couldn't have come at a more perfect time!"

Renee Swope, best-selling author of *A Confident Heart*

"*Whispers of Rest* is a wonderful resource to detox from life's busyness or hurts while learning how to practice good soul care. It provides inspirational tips to bring deeper intimacy with God and becoming renewed daily."

Stephen Arterburn, *New York Times* bestselling author of *Take Back Your Life*, Founder of New Life Ministries and radio talk-show host of *New Life Live!*

"There are so many ways that I love this book. I adore Bonnie's gentle approach to invite the one who has been walking with Jesus for decades as well as the spiritual novice. She has made room at the table for each of us to have an encounter with the Living God in a new, fresh and surprising way using the most ancient of practices. *Whispers of Rest* will be a part of my regular rotation of devotionals. Highly recommended."

Kathi Lipp, best-selling author of *Overwhelmed* and *Clutter Free*

"Bonnie has a beautiful gift of creating quiet spaces where men and women can encounter God. Using truth and scripture to point us to Him, Bonnie invites us to rest."

Michele Cushatt, author of *I Am: A 60-day Journey To Knowing Who You Are Because of Who He Is*

"In our noisy, nonstop life of busy, Bonnie Gray's *Whispers of Rest* is a balm for soul. Treasure this book as I have."

Claire Diaz-Ortiz, author of *Design Your Day* and entrepreneur, ClaireDiazOrtiz.com

whispers
of
rest

⟿ ⟿ ⟿

40 Days of God's Love to
Revitalize Your Soul

Bonnie Gray

Faith
Words

New York   Nashville

FaithWords
Hachette Book Group
1290 Avenue of the Americas, New York, NY 10104
faithwords.com
twitter.com/faithwords

First Edition: May 2017

FaithWords is a division of Hachette Book Group, Inc. The FaithWords name and logo are trademarks of Hachette Book Group, Inc.

The publisher is not responsible for websites (or their content) that are not owned by the publisher.

The Hachette Speakers Bureau provides a wide range of authors for speaking events. To find out more, go to www.hachettespeakersbureau.com or call (866) 376-6591.

Library of Congress Cataloging-in-Publication Data has been applied for.

ISBN: 978-1-4555-9820-5 (trade paperback), 978-1-4555-9821-2 (ebook)

Printed in the United States of America

LSC-H

10 9 8 7 6 5

To Jesus —

*my North Star whose loving whispers of rest healed my heart
and restored my spark.*

To Eric —

my beloved whose voice of love is a sheltering tree.

To Josh and Caleb

because you are beloved and beautiful to Mommy.

And to my Kindred Readers

whose living stories shine God's beauty each day.

Contents

Hello

Life has gotten too noisy. My heart feels frayed.

Like a child planting a seed and forgetting where she placed it, I wonder if anything beautiful and tender can break through the soil of my heart again. I try to pray, but sometimes it's hard to find the words.

I need God, though, and I want to feel close to Him again. Like I did as a child.

And then I remember. There are whispers of love and peace waiting to hold me if I am willing to take a moment. To stop. Draw close. And listen.

And so I do, through a daily practice.

Ever feel this way, this longing to draw close and be known?

If you deeply desire to feel the touch of God's voice fall fresh on your soul...

If you ache for the tenderness of an intimate conversation with the One who calls you His...

If you'd like to be embraced by the stillness of God's presence—to return to your First Love and let Him captivate your heart the way a sunrise leans into a new day...

If you'd like to experience God in simple ways again...

This forty-day journey of the soul is for you.

There's something special about forty. In forty days, Jesus found his voice in the wilderness intertwined with God's words. In forty weeks, the seed of life in a woman's womb transforms into flesh, a baby with a heartbeat and a name. For forty years, God whispered "Good morning" by sending manna falling like dew, nourishing the body and soul.

A lot can happen in forty days. A new rhythm. A new heart.

It's about finding your spark again. To be the Beloved. Just as you are.

Whispers of Rest is a life-giving, forty-day devotional detox for your soul, far from the noise and demands of everyday life—refreshing your spirit with simple, powerful affirmations of God's love, paired with intimate reflection questions and easy-to-enjoy practical challenges and tips.

This forty-day devotional journey reflects the very same quest I took to renew my heart with God's whispers again. To return to my First Love. To enjoy simply being with God. And allowing Him to be with me.

Through this soulful, practical, Scripture-based guide, you'll experience prayer in a new and fresh way, reigniting your heart with God's love and rest.

So what would happen if every day—for the next forty days—you soaked in God's voice of love as He intimately whispered words of rest just for you?

Let me show you what I mean . . .

Introduction

"First, silence makes us pilgrims. Secondly, silence guards the fire within. Thirdly, silence teaches us to speak."

HENRI NOUWEN

When I was a little girl, I loved watching the shadows dance along the walls of my bedroom.

You might think they were the arms of a willow tree gently swaying across my window in the breeze. But the shadows that fluttered like an old silent movie reel, in fact, came from the headlights of cars streaming behind our two-bedroom duplex. Sometimes, after reading late into the night, I'd walk on my lumpy mattress over to the window, pull back the curtains, stand there pressed up close, and with my breath fogging the windowpane, I would look for the glow of the moonlight.

I'd find that moon somewhere in the arc of its ascent into the skies. If it was a clear night, I'd see a star. Maybe two. In that hushed moment, I felt something beautiful. Peaceful.

I know beauty isn't usually considered to be a feeling, but that's how it seemed to me. Sometimes a song would come to mind and I'd sing it softly. Most of the time, I'd rest there, staring into the night, dark as molasses stretched across the heavens, until the stars twinkled back.

Something about that quiet moment made me feel close to

God. Whatever was bothering me or made me happy would spill out. I would confide to God about what happened during the day. *I would share my most hidden thoughts and dreams, fears and worries.*

In the stillness of a hushed conversation, prompted by seeing the beauty of the stars twinkling in the night sky, God would soothe my heart with words of love and peace—*God's whispers of rest.*

New Journey of the Heart

I didn't know then as a child that something as ordinary as seeing the moon through my window would become an anchor to my soul later on, when I became an adult and my world became overrun by stress and anxiety. I struggled to sleep and felt a weariness I couldn't shake. My heart felt restless and, tossed by a sea of critical voices, paralyzed by overanalyzing and second-guessing myself.

I lost my spark. I lost the spring in my step and the song in my heart. Peace and joy were missing. I was surviving and competent, but deep in my soul I felt tired and uninspired. I knew life was supposed to be beautiful because God loved me, but I didn't *feel* like life was beautiful, even though I was thankful for everything God had done in my life.

Losing my joy made me feel ashamed, until God's whispers of rest loved me back to life. God wasn't ashamed of my need. *God understood my longing for beauty, peace, and intimacy—and He understands your heart, too.*

Eventually, when my boys were still young, I sought the help of a Christian therapist to navigate the mysteries of my soul and my story. *And I began a new journey of the heart—and was at last able to hear God's whispers of love and peace again.*

Finding Your Spark: God's Beloved

To heal, I uncovered some painful memories. But some of the most beautiful moments in my life also returned to me in the process—times when I felt most powerfully touched by God's presence. Whenever I felt emotionally overwhelmed, I would think on those moments, and God's words would bring me back to a place of love and peace.

This book is a collection of God's most beautiful whispers of rest uncovered during my three-year journey. *Using this guidebook, you will experience greater peace and discover who God truly made you to be—His Beloved. You will hear God's voice in new ways, experience His love more intimately, and revitalize your soul using simple tools of soul care to refresh your body and spirit.* You will find your voice, rediscover your dreams, and find your spark of joy again.

God's whispers of rest healed me and restored my spark. *God restored the joy.* You know, that glow inside you when you feel utterly safe, special, and known—that makes you feel alive, that all is right in the world—*that you are right in the world?*

And the beautiful news is this: This journey of rest will refresh your spirit with the renewing touch of God's love and bring back your spark, too. To be God's Beloved.

What began as a necessity for my healing has now become a daily practice to listen and refresh my heart, held gently in God's arms. And now together as kindred between these pages, we'll see God's sweet words making us fresh and new, day by day.

I believe God's whispers of rest are meant for you, too.

"Draw near to God and He will draw near to you."

JAMES 4:8

A Beautiful Invitation

I invite you to engage your heart and embark on a *forty-day journey* to:

- *Refresh an intimacy with God in your prayer life.*
- *Revitalize your soul with His words of love and peace for you each day.*

To hear God's intimate voice of love is about being vulnerable. It's about having conversations and sharing stories with God that you've kept quiet. To receive. To confide and pray. *It's about becoming the Beloved—and finding your spark again.*

And I feel so honored to be your guide on this beautiful journey.

How to Use This Book

Finding God's whispers for you is like going on a beautiful hike. In that spirit, this forty-day devotional journey is written like a trail guide so you can experience beautiful moments with God every day in two ways. First, you will hear God's intimate, personal words to you each day, reminding you how beloved you are. And second, you will express your heart in return, both to God in private conversation and with friends as you journey with them through this book.

Each day, we will travel to a different destination of your soul. At each stop, you'll be invited *to experience God as you*:

1. *Read:* Read God's story in "God's Whispers to You," inspired by Scripture.
2. *Reflect:* Reflect on your story with God, using journaling prompts.

3. *Pray & Rest:* Pray, draw near to God, and quiet your heart to focus on Him.

You'll need just three things:

> *a journal*
> *a quiet corner where you can't be interrupted*
> *desire*

By following this forty-day journey—to *read, reflect, pray and rest*—you'll experience the ancient method of praying with Scripture known in Latin as *Lectio Divina*, which simply means "divine reading." In this beautiful method developed in early Christian history, God's voice comes intimately alive, in personal ways.

It's a way of reading the Scriptures slowly, to listen to God with our hearts and experience His peace and presence. This rhythm will bring you *to a place of resting in God*, of letting God's whispers dwell in you and become a desire to know Him more intimately and be known in return. *As you do, your desire will become prayer.*

Journey Mercies

Whenever I go on a hike, I love packing snacks (usually including chocolate). Here are some goodies for our journey each day:

- *Inspirational Quotes and Scriptures:* Powerful words of affirmation.
- *A Simple Prayer Practice:* Enjoy a unique daily prayer prompt to deepen intimacy with God, inspired by classic Christian devotional practices.

- *A Prayer for the Day:* An encouraging prayer for your heart.
- *A One Word Prayer:* A one word touchstone from Scripture to experience God's presence throughout the day.
- *Daily Beloved Challenge:* Take simple soul care actions to brighten your day and nurture your well-being.
- *Soul Care Trail Notes:* Practical tips and interesting studies to reduce stress and refresh your body and spirit.

The truth is, we're all a little stressed on the journey of life. But armed with this easy, accessible list of forty inspiring things you can do anytime, you will create space for your soul to breathe and revitalize your soul with God's love. You will reduce stress and give yourself a much-needed break from a hectic life!

The Destination: Experience Jesus More Intimately

"This hope we have as an anchor of the soul,
a hope both sure and steadfast...
where Jesus has entered."   HEBREWS 6:19–20

God's whispers of rest guide us to a beautiful destination of hope, an anchor for the soul in a stress-filled world. Our destination for this journey isn't some*thing*, but *Someone*. Our hope is *Jesus*. Like an anchor, each day's *One Word* prayer returns you to Jesus. You will experience Jesus more intimately—and find your spirit and mind renewed with joy and peace, day by day, just as the Scriptures promise.

The Most Beautiful Treasure: Your Own Collection

By the end of forty days, if you enjoy journaling, you will be holding the most beautiful treasure in your hands when we finish: *your own collection of the most intimate prayers and conversations between you and Jesus* uncovered during this special journey of the soul.

Jesus invites you to draw closer, to rest and let him love you more deeply. Jesus whispers:

> *I'm here. In the quiet. Loving you. Holding you.*
> *In the sanctuary of your most private moments,*
> *your heart becomes my home.*
> *I will be an anchor for your soul. I will be your hope.*

It's His promise. You can experience God's presence, fresh and new. *Today.*

Open your heart and listen. Look and see. Stop and breathe.

Let God hold your heart, like the moon rising to meet the stars at night and the sun waking to cast its rays of color into a new day. Together, let's return to who we were always created to be.

Let's be the Beloved. God's Beloved.

And as we take this journey together, I'm praying you will be inspired with new courage and ideas to step out and shine as God's Beloved!

More Beauty: Journey in Community

We live in a disconnected culture that is dominated by busyness and social media, and we're surrounded by pressures to constantly perform. Yet Jesus came to us as a person, with an actual voice that said, "Hello," and "I understand," with eyes that laughed and even cried. Jesus was real and he was vulnerable.

We need each other. That was really what Jesus was saying as he spent time with friends—as he told his stories. *Jesus became known.*

So I encourage you to use this guide in two ways:

1. Enjoy it during your personal devotional time, *and*
2. Read it together with other people in a group.

Read this book with friends once a week, to share your new discoveries. *Life is so much more beautiful when we journey with others.* I've designed the journaling prompts to spark conversation, to share your heart and experiences with each other. By going on this forty-day journey with friends, you will partake in something incredibly real together: *your stories*, for your mutual encouragement and joy.

You and me. We need the beauty and warmth of a kindred spirit to share our stories. As we do, we find the courage and refreshment that comes only from being vulnerable in community.

We become real. We become known. We become the Beloved.

Let us begin.

whispers
of
rest

PART ONE

Being the Beloved

— ❧ ❧ ❧ —

Embrace Your True Identity
as God's Beloved

Your journey to revitalize your soul
begins by hearing God gently whisper,
You are my Beloved.
And by whispering *Yes* in return.

This first set of devotionals
invites you to *embrace your true identity.*
God is naming you.
He calls you *Beloved.*

"You are my beloved… In you, I take delight."

MARK 1:11

DAY 1

Yes

Don't be afraid. Set your heart free.

Like the sun rising to touch the arms of a winter tree,
God gently whispers,
Don't be afraid. I love you forever.
Make me yours today.

Leave the safety of what you know and
let God's love be your safety instead.
Begin a new journey.
Be the Beloved. Say yes.

"I run in the path of your commands for you have set my
heart free." PSALM 119:32

✑ ✑ ✑

"Define yourself radically as one beloved by God. This is the true self. Every other identity is illusion."

BRENNAN MANNING

Sometimes, the world can make you feel small. It can be a crowded place, so many voices. Loud. *Insistent* that you have something to show. For who you are. And what you have to offer.

What you hold in your heart—faith, hope, and love—can feel inadequate.

As you see what others are offering, you may be tempted to put your hopes and dreams back in your pocket. And close the door of your heart to the possibility of who you really are.

Don't listen to those voices. Step closer to the One Voice who knows you.

Listen to the One who saw you the very moment you were born. When you broke into this world, helpless, eyes shut, fingers balled up in trembling fists, lungs blaring with hungry cries, God saw you. And loved you. Completely.

You are *exactly* the way God dreamed of you when He made you lovingly in the secret place. You are still that same Beloved. When He looks straight into the secret places within you, God sees the real you.

It was how Jesus might have felt standing at a lake, with crowds of people pressing against him—looking for someone to call friend.

READ GOD'S STORY

It was there along the shore, in Luke 5:1–10, that Jesus turned from the noise of the crowd and noticed something in the distance: two boats floating at the edge. *Empty.*

Jesus saw.

The fishermen were dragging their boats back onto the sand. They had given up. They were washing their nets. They had worked hard all night. Yet, there was no catch. It was there, in the middle of their everyday work, Jesus told them what he'd been waiting all his life to say face-to-face: *Come follow me.*

Jesus chooses us the way he chose his first confidants, his disciples. This friendship begins the way falling in love finds us. *It comes unexpectedly.*

The fishermen had caught nothing. Their nets were empty.

Then, Jesus called them to a miraculous way of filling them with fish: *Go deeper and let down your nets.* And their nets were filled to overflowing.

But then something radical happened next. *Jesus called them away from that way of life.* Jesus was calling them to leave something they all had *a lot of experience* doing—and instead *say yes* to something they had *no experience* doing.

When Jesus calls us into deeper intimacy, he says, "Don't be afraid. I will do it with you."

Jesus calls us to leave behind our "nets" of competence and instead experience being the Beloved—with him.

Will you say yes to this new journey?

Good Enough?

Even when Jesus shows Peter he cares for his needs by filling his nets, Peter is afraid. "Go away from me Lord...I am a sinful man!" (Luke 5:8).

Peter doesn't think he's good enough. Isn't that how we often feel when God invites us to something beautiful and real? Let Jesus' words to Peter become yours today: "Don't be afraid. From now on, you will fish for people" (Luke 5:10).

In other words, Jesus is saying:

What I want is your heart. I see what no one else sees: the beautiful things I want to give you—and to others—through you.

How did the disciples respond to Jesus' invitation? The scene at the sea ends by showing us what they did—

Immediately they left their nets and *followed* Him...
Immediately they left the boat
and *followed* Him.   MATTHEW 4:20-20

☞ *God's Whispers to You*

Imagine Jesus noticing you now, moving close, gently placing his hand on yours, to whisper these words:

Beloved,
Don't be afraid. You don't have to try so hard.
Lay down your burdens. Let me take them from you.
So that you can run free.
You're my Beloved.
Come with me to a new way of living.
Say yes. I will set your heart free.

God's whispers are calling you to *experience Him* more than what you can *do* for Him on this journey. Jesus wants you to say *YES to surrendering your heart*, rather than putting your safety into executing a plan.

Peter's life previously *depended on his ability to provide for himself—by what he could do.* Where his experience, skills, tools—even his timetable—and expertise guided him. Now, Jesus was calling Peter to *experience a journey of promise and possibilities*—where God's presence would guide *who he would become* as the Beloved.

Imagine now the future of promise and possibility waiting for you *as God's Beloved.*

✑ *A Prayer for Today:*
When You Want to Say Yes

"I run in the path of your commands for you have set my heart free." PSALM 119:32

Dear Jesus,
Help me to let go of my empty nets and hold on to you instead.
Even though I'm afraid, help me to say yes to you.
I want to follow you wherever you call me to go.
I don't want to try so hard anymore. Set my heart free.
Amen.

Give Yourself Permission: Say yes. Begin a new journey with Jesus. Let go of your nets. Set your heart free.

REFLECT ON YOUR STORY

1. *How is Jesus unexpectedly prompting your heart to say YES to something new and unknown—and leave something old and familiar?*

2. *What is the net you've been holding on to? What is holding you back?*

3. *What do you need to let go of in order to follow Jesus ahead—people, places, routines, possessions, expectations, roles, or responsibilities?*

PRAY & REST

A SIMPLE PRACTICE: PRAYER IS CONVERSATION

One Word Prayer is a simple way to experience what pastor and author Timothy Keller shares in his book *Prayer:* "Prayer is *continuing a conversation* that God has started through his Word and his grace, which eventually becomes a full *encounter* with him."

Reflect on a word or phrase that draws your attention. Then use it as a prayer prompt to spark a *conversation* with God.

How: Sit relaxed. Close your eyes. Use today's One Word Prayer, *YES*, as a gentle focus. What feelings, questions, or thoughts emerge? Share them now with Jesus. (You can also choose your own One Word from Luke 5:1–10, Psalm 119:32, or Matthew 4:20–22.)

Write your One Word Prayer here and share why it's meaningful to you:

━━━━ *◿ ◿ ◿* ━━━━

TODAY'S BELOVED CHALLENGE

Journal for Ten Minutes
Invite Jesus into your world.

Make the space to *say yes* to God. Allow your heart to be set free.

SOUL CARE TRAIL NOTES

Journaling Increases Happiness

Sometimes it's hard to hear God's voice when we're overwhelmed by everyday stresses. *You can journal.* Invite Jesus to enter *your* world. Have a conversation with him on the page.

Research in a *New York Times* article shows how the power of writing your personal story lowers anxiety, leads to behavioral changes, and improves happiness. Just ten to fifteen minutes of expressive writing makes a difference! *"For the word of God is living and active...It penetrates dividing soul and spirit"* (Hebrews 4:12). The "word" is the Greek word *logos*—translated as "living voice" or "story." God uses everything living to speak to us.

When we journal our stories with God, we give Him space to rewrite our stories. Don't you get *ah-ha* moments as you write?

DAY 2

Confide

Lean into me. Confide in me.

Today, when stress grips you
and you're tempted to retreat into busyness, stop.
Be still and breathe.

Step away and open your heart
to the beauty of God's grace instead.
Hear Jesus whisper,
Lean into me. Let me love you.
Confide in me.

*"If I make my bed in the depths, you are there…if I settle
on the far side of the sea, even there…your right hand
will hold me."* PSALM 139:8–10

When I was a little girl, I dreamed of living somewhere quiet, beautiful and spacious. I loved watching the TV show *Little House on the Prairie*, especially the opening scene, when Ma and Pa would stop their horse-drawn carriage and the girls would roll out of the wagon like minimarshmallows, running downhill on the grass, golden hair wisping behind, like kites doing somersaults in the sky.

I did not grow up like that. I grew up in an eight-hundred-square-foot duplex unit in the middle of a busy intersection in Silicon Valley. There weren't that many windows in our home, and on the ones we had, we kept the curtain closed. I didn't grow up with Pa at home, and my ma was not was like Mrs. Ingalls. Yet deep in my heart, something about the wide, open spaces called to me.

I didn't go on my first hike until I was in fifth grade. That was the year our class went to Science Camp. I boarded a big yellow school bus lugging a sleeping bag borrowed from my aunt, with my pillow rolled in between, like pigs in a blanket, and headed for the Saratoga Mountains. Big redwood trees, lining the narrow driveway our bus tottered down to camp, reached in through our windows with their branches, tickling us as we brushed past them.

Even the air smelled different. As I jumped off the bus with giggling classmates, I felt what half-pint Laura Ingalls might have felt. Happy. Free. I looked up at the trees and felt small and safe. I could breathe.

Our camp counselors said the big event was the night hike. We gathered at the trailhead after sunset, hyped with adrenaline. But everyone fell stone silent once we learned we would be sent hiking *alone* from point A to point B. In the dark.

11

We were told to walk quietly. But if we got scared, all we needed to do was to call out. Camp counselors stationed at different points along the trail would help us.

That night was one of the most beautiful nights I have ever experienced. The light foliage felt like a soft carpet on the trail. I wasn't afraid. The stars glimmered between the lattice rooftops of the Redwoods.

The deeper I journeyed into the trail, something beautiful and unexpected happened. *I began to see in the dark.*

READ GOD'S STORY

Looking back, today I'm reminded of what the Psalmist whispered to God,

> *"If I say, 'Surely the darkness will overwhelm me,*
> *And the light around me will be night,'*
> *Even the darkness is not dark to you,*
> *And the night is as bright as the day. Darkness and light*
> *are alike to you. For you formed my inward parts; you*
> *wove me in my mother's womb."*   PSALM 139:11–13

God sees us in the dark. If we remember there is Someone close, a Voice of Love whispering to us, our spiritual eyes can adjust and we begin to see the beauty of the journey we're on.

Lean into me. Let me love you. Confide in me.

We may not know the way, but the God who loves you not only knows *the* way—but He intimately knows *your* way.

Since you and I were little girls, we've trained ourselves to be resourceful. We don't want to rely on anyone. We are educated and many of us are self-taught.

It's a strength that's made us resilient, but there is a side effect: the loss of vulnerability. We travel unknown. We don't feel comfortable letting someone in on our doubts and questions. We confide in others, but only after we've figured things out—bleeding over into our conversations with God.

Holding back our hearts affects our relationship with God and with others. It even affects our prayers. We incorrectly think having faith means waiting to pray until we no longer feel uncertain about God, ourselves, or our purpose. We're afraid God sees us the way our peers might judge us—by our confidence, progress, or productivity.

The truth is we often wait for clarity. But God wants us to confide in Him about the actual journey—and how we're doing on it—more than getting to the destination. *Like stars glimmering at rest in the night, faith is a quiet, hushed conversation with God—intimately confiding what we desire and fear.*

Confiding in God is a radical movement of the heart, allowing ourselves to be known, to become the Beloved.

✒ *God's Whispers to You*

Today, if you're feeling uncertain about how you feel, hear God's whisper to you:

Beloved,
I see you. I won't leave or forsake you.
Call out for me. And I'll take your hand.
I'll turn the darkness into a place of rest,
lit by my love for you.
Lean into me. Let me love you. Confide in me.

When you find yourself falling between moments of confidence and then confusion in the course of a day, don't be alarmed. We were never meant to journey alone. God is with us. In the day *and* in the night.

✏ *A Prayer for Today:*
When You Feel Uncertain

"If I make my bed in the depths, you are there…if I settle on the far side of the sea, even there…your right hand will hold me."   PSALM 139:8–10

Thank you, Jesus.
For walking with me. Even in the dark.
Help me remember what you told me in the daylight.

Give me eyes to see you now. So I can lean into you.
Help me call out and confide in you when I can't see ahead.
So I can walk as your Beloved today.
Amen.

Give Yourself Permission: Honestly tell Jesus how you're feeling. Be vulnerable about your uncertainties. Ask for help. Enjoy a walk in nature.

REFLECT ON YOUR STORY

1. *What uncertainties circle your heart but you've kept unspoken?*

2. *What is a beautiful moment you experienced in nature that God used to touch your heart?*

3. *What One Word from Scripture catches your attention today?*

PRAY & REST

A SIMPLE PRACTICE: PRAYER IS AN HONEST CONVERSATION

Max Lucado once shared that prayer must be an honest conversation with God and not a repetitive act: "I don't pray for long periods of time...my prayers are relatively brief. The times I really feel blessed through prayer is when my prayers are sincere—when I kind of think through what I'm going through, or I'm going through a hard time and I use that prayer to talk to God about everything."

For today's prayer, have an honest conversation with God. Set everything aside now. Today's One Word is *CONFIDE*. Finish these sentences to confide in God.

Dear God, I've been quiet about this, but what I really want is . . .

What's really hard for me right now is . . .

Close your eyes. Pray. Confide in Jesus now. As friend to friend.

TODAY'S BELOVED CHALLENGE

Take a Ten-Minute Prayer Walk
Have an honest conversation with God.

Rest in the certainty that your journey—that *you*—are known and loved. Confide.

SOUL CARE TRAIL NOTES

Walking in Nature Refreshes You

Uncertainty triggers feelings of fear and stress. *But research shows that just ten minutes of walking in nature refreshes you, boosting your mood and helping with anxiety, depression in schoolwork, work, and everyday life.*

Praying doesn't need to happen while sitting in your home. My favorite time to pray happens every morning after I drop my boys off at school and take a walk on a trail. (It may be in the afternoon or evening for you.) It's so rejuvenating.

Take a walk outside and let God touch you. Take the pressure off yourself to find words to pray. No need to speak. You can spend your prayer time simply resting in God's presence in nature, letting Him refresh you. The most intimate conversations happen spontaneously when you finally have space to breathe.

Breathe

Be beloved, not busy. Come away with me.

Today, you and I have a choice:
We can stop.
Be still and breathe.

Rest with Jesus and hear him whisper,
Be beloved, not busy.
Come away with me. Today.

"Come away with me by yourselves to a quiet place and
rest awhile."   MARK 6:31

"Each of us needs to withdraw from the cares which will not withdraw from us." MAYA ANGELOU

We'd never been to the Point Reyes Lighthouse. To jump-start the new year, my husband, Eric, and I took our two boys to go see it. But on the drive to the lighthouse, all we saw were miles of rocky, empty terrain. There were no trees.

It all looked desolate and boring. *Nothing to see here.*

"Let's just take some pictures and leave," I told Eric. I didn't want to waste time. I wanted go back to Muir Woods, where we visited the day before. *I wanted to go back to what was known.*

"Look, Mom!" six-year-old Caleb and ten-year-old Josh shouted, pointing ahead. The road started climbing uphill. "It looks like we're going to fall off a cliff!"

"It just looks that way," I answered. "You'll see. The road doesn't end. We're too far now to see ahead."

Then, our car stopped at the top of hill. And I was stunned.

As far as my eye could see, miles and miles of beaches—all uninterrupted by trees—stretched out like a crescent moon, as the ocean cascaded onto the sand in a continuous spray, like Olympic swimmers digging powerful strokes across the sea.

As we took the boys on a beautiful hike down to the lighthouse, I was reminded by the waves returning to shore, the blue skies shining off the cliffs—as we watched gray whales breaching in migration across the lighthouse—*everything beautiful moves by God's invitation.*

So I asked myself: *What if all my busyness was only leading me back to what I knew, while God was at work in all His glory creating something beautiful and new?* Rather than striving to please, to belong or avoid hurt, what is the more restful journey that God is inviting me into, to step out in faith and experience with Him?

Am I moving by God's invitation or by my striving?

It struck me like lightning. **If we turned back to only what we know, we would miss out on the beautiful journey God has for us now.**

It's easier to get pulled away by busyness and stress. But busyness takes a toll on us. We rush from one thing to the next. Yet, with every checklist we complete, there is a cost. *Checklists never end.*

Unless we step away and rest, unless we allow God to restore and revitalize us, we become dangerously busy. Depleted and diminished in our capacity:

to feel our emotions,

to hear God's whispers,

to be present with others,

to be who we were created to be: simply beloved.

We need to time to refresh, even if it initially appears barren or feels wasteful.

Maybe living one restful moment at a time—to receive just one word of love from Jesus every day—*leads us to a completely different, life-giving destination* than the one we'd reach with the plans we chart for ourselves, which leads only to more busyness.

What if God's plan for us is not to be more busy, but to be more loved?

READ GOD'S STORY

Listen to Jesus' invitation to you now, the one he offered to his disciples:

> *"Come away with me by yourselves*
> *to a quiet place and rest awhile."*   MARK 6:31

That day was so busy, the Scriptures tell us, they didn't have time to eat. The crowds were following them. So many people in need, so many things to do, so many things left unsaid.

Yet Jesus invites his disciples to step away. No more doing or meeting needs. *They even had to escape by boat to get away.*

In the same way, Jesus today says us, "*You* are worth it." We need to unplug and get rejuvenated.

What you see as a barren, blank space in your schedule, God uses to bring beauty into your day—like waves washing over the sand. God wants to fill your calendar with peace and joy. He wants to refill *you.*

Could Jesus be giving you permission to step away by "boat"—or by some radical, unexpected way—to leave the "crowds" in your world and unplug from busyness?

✐ *God's Whispers to You*

Beloved,
You are worth it.
Listen to my whispers for you.
Be still and breathe.

Let me love you with the awe-inspiring beauty I've created in nature for you—in the breathtaking ocean waves that refresh your spirit, the sweet birdsong that sings the hope of my care, the warmth of sunshine on your shoulder, or the magnificent shelter in the arms of a quiet tree.

Dare to step away. Unplug.
Come away with me.
Rest awhile. With me. Today.

✐ A Prayer for Today:
When You Feel Overwhelmed

*"Come away with me by yourselves
to a quiet place and rest awhile."*   MARK 6:31

*Dear Jesus,
I want to be restored. Refreshed.
Give me courage to choose beauty.
Like waves returning the sand, have your way in me.*

*Help me step away.
I choose to be beloved, not busy.
To rest awhile with you. Today.
Amen.*

Give Yourself Permission: Step away for some *Me Time*. Stop pouring out. Enjoy what fills you up.

REFLECT ON YOUR STORY

1. *How can you step away to refresh your soul with God? What would your Me Time look like?*

2. *Where do you experience God's peace and rest? What landscape speaks to you the most—beach, mountain, the woods, or desert?*

3. *What One Word in today's Scripture speaks to you today?*

PRAY & REST

A SIMPLE PRACTICE: BREATH PRAYERS

A *Breath Prayer* is a simple way to pray using the natural rhythm of your breathing. Deep breathing oxygenates your brain and reenergizes you. Now, breath prayers will oxygenate your soul with God's presence and bring you calm.

The Breath Prayer is a contemplative prayer practiced by the early church to experience God's peace, practice the presence of God, and "pray without ceasing."

How to Pray a Breath Prayer

1. Close your eyes and meditate on a Bible verse, as a prompt to meet with God. *"Come away with me by yourselves to a quiet place and rest awhile"* (Mark 6:31).
2. Pray to God silently. Inhale, whispering God's name. Then, exhale your two- or three-word request, gratitude, or just share how you feel.

   For example:
   Jesus. *Breathe in—opening your heart, be present to Him.*
   Help me. *Breathe out—allowing God to touch you.*
   God, I need you.   *Jesus, thank you.*
   Heavenly Father, guide me.   *Lord, I'm listening.*

3. Continue breathing deeply. Rest. If you can enjoy the quiet for five to ten minutes, you'll enjoy the destressing benefits of meditation, bringing calm to your mind. As your thoughts wander, gently return to your breath prayer. Enjoy the stillness.

"Be still and know that I am God."   PSALM 46:10

Pray Your Breath Prayer

Invite Jesus in. Share what the experience feels like for you. Today's One Word Prayer is *BREATHE*. *Write your Breath Prayer here:*

TODAY'S BELOVED CHALLENGE

Take a Photo of Something Beautiful
Breathe. Observe. Be still and listen to God.

Stop with God and notice what's beautiful. Taking pictures can be your time of meditation with Him. Rest.

SOUL CARE TRAIL NOTES

Taking Photos Helps You Relax

When we step away from busyness, we become free to rest and be refreshed. Pastor and author Rick Warren says, "Busyness doesn't prove significance. Activity isn't productivity. A busy life can be a barren life. Be still and listen to God."

Today, when stress grips you and you're tempted to solve it by being busy, step away and enjoy beauty with God instead. *Take a photo of what's beautiful to you. Taking pictures can be your time of meditation.*

Research shows creative activities like photography help you relax, lowering your stress levels, leaving you feeling mentally clear and calm. Taking a photo disrupts the usual flow of worrisome thoughts or juggling lists. It gives your brain a mental break to focus on something new and offers the calming benefits of meditation.

Come

Let me be your hiding place.
Rest in my arms today.

God hears your unanswered prayers.
He's always listening,
loving you just as you are.

You can be weary. You can rest.
Jesus tenderly whispers,
Come to me. Let me be your hiding place.
Rest in my arms today.

"For you are my hiding place... You surround me with
songs of deliverance."   PSALM 32:7

"One day spent with someone you love can change everything."
MITCH ALBOM

I didn't know that I was hiding. I've always been good at praying. Or so I thought.

My dad left when I was seven. I've always looked to God as my Father, my provider. What I didn't realize is that God wants to be more than just my provider. God longs to be my soul's confidant—deep where I feel lonely, where I struggle to receive and make space for myself.

Loneliness is something I usually cover up by getting things done. It looks good, because I'm well rewarded for checking boxes and being productive. Even in ministry.

But at the end of the day, even though I've accomplished a lot, I don't feel like I've fully lived. Because I didn't make space for what I really want: *to be known.* I did not nurture my soul with God.

I find it easier to take care of others and get things done for God, rather than be vulnerable with my needs. *But God is showing me that prayer is an intimate soul conversation to allow me to loved and known, rather than a spiritual transaction to be made better.*

Praying touches the part of me that is in process, uncertain, full of questions and doubts. That is why praying is hard to do. And when I don't know how to pray, it makes me feel ashamed.

Do you ever feel this way? Do you find yourself longing for God's touch, yet you don't feel like praying—or can't find the words?

Jesus understands. While others may turn away, he steps closer.

READ GOD'S STORY

Listen now, as Jesus reaches for your hand to whisper:

"Come to me,
all of you who are weary and carry heavy burdens,
and I will give you rest.

Are you tired? Worn out? Burned out on religion?
Get away with me and you'll recover your life.
I'll show you how to take a real rest.
Walk with me... Watch how I do it.
Learn the unforced rhythms of grace.
I won't lay anything heavy or ill fitting on you.
Keep company with me,
and you will learn to live freely and lightly.

For I am gentle and humble in heart
and you will find rest for your souls."   MATTHEW 11:28–29

Notice Jesus doesn't say, "Come to me strong, cheerful, without worries." We're invited to come to him *weary*—whether confused, numb, anxious, angry, or stressed. Jesus tells us to simply come. *Imperfectly his.* As we are.

If we wait until we are better or stronger, or until we no longer struggle, we will never need faith—or ever taste the sweetness of being held and loved.

Even though Scripture encourages us to simply come to Jesus as we are, our Christian church culture often gives the opposite message. Our desert prayer times are often met with well-meaning encouragement like, "Relationship with God isn't a feeling." Although partially true, this can dehumanize our connection with God. The Psalmist reminds us that there are no easy answers. "He himself knows our frame; He is mindful that we are but dust" (Psalm 103:14).

Sometimes, it takes more faith to tell God we don't know what or how to pray—rather than praying for the faith to pray like we once did.

God's Nearness

Sometimes, even though we know God is with us, we can't feel His touch. *We need to let God into our messy, unorganized thoughts—our unabashed excitement, dreams and desires, and our feelings of confusion.* Sometimes, we need to voice the questions we'd rather avoid. We need to let God in.

When the Psalmist David wakes up, he says,

> *"In the morning, Lord, you hear my voice.*
> *I direct my prayer to you and I wait expectantly*
> *for you."* PSALM 5:3

David didn't hold back his thoughts. *David waited expectantly— not for the answers, but for God's nearness.*

✐ *God's Whispers to You*

Jesus understands our weariness. See his loving gaze fall on you now.

Beloved,
Lay your heartbeat close to mine.
You don't have to be strong enough.
You can rest here with me.

Let me be your hiding place.
Be my Beloved.
Come. Rest in my arms today.

Rest your heart in the One who is in control of your heart and your destiny.

✍ *A Prayer for Today:*
When You Carry a Heavy Burden

"But as for me, the nearness of God is my good;
I have made the Lord God my refuge."   PSALM 73:28

Dear Jesus,
I don't know how not to be in control.
And yet you still call me to come. As I am.

Help me, Jesus,
to trust you.
I lay it all down now.

Thank you for never giving up on me,
and for quietly waiting for me to let you love me. Today.
Amen.

Whatever you are carrying, lay it down. Lay down everything you were never intended to carry, friend. *There is no burden too heavy that God cannot carry for you.*

Cast those burdens on the One who hears your voice and calls you Beloved.

Rather than being harder on yourself when you feel stressed, nurture the one Jesus carries close to his heart—*you.*

Give Yourself Permission: Prioritize your well-being. Accept your feelings. Let go of whatever is too heavy for you. Do what brings you physical or emotional rest. Be kind to yourself.

REFLECT ON YOUR STORY

1. *What helps you to feel close to God?*

2. *How has your prayer life changed throughout the years? What are your questions about prayer? What makes prayer easy or difficult?*

3. *What One Word is God whispering to your heart today?*

PRAY & REST

A SIMPLE PRACTICE: LETTER MEDITATION

Teresa of Ávila, a Carmelite nun in the sixteenth century, describes the journey to pray and experience God intimately in her book *Interior Castle*, "The important thing is *not to think much* but to *love much*; and so do that which best stirs you to love."

When I'm overthinking and stressed, writing a letter to Jesus helps me come to him and open my heart.

Today, write a letter to Jesus as your contemplative prayer. Write your letter as stream of consciousness, unfiltered. Use today's One Word Prayer, *COME*, as a writing prompt. Let God touch you as you write.

Dear Jesus . . .

───── 🖊 🖊 🖊 ─────

TODAY'S BELOVED CHALLENGE

Write a Letter to Someone You Love
Share what you appreciate.
Mail it or tuck it somewhere fun to be found.

Take ten minutes. Think of someone who brings joy or love to your life. They are God's presence to you. Write a letter letting them know.

SOUL CARE TRAIL NOTES

Letter Writing Counters Stress

We are such strong thinkers. Sometimes it leads us to easily ruminate, which means to obsess about situations or relationships, leaving us feeling depressed or anxious. One way to reduce rumination is by enjoying activities that foster positive thoughts.

Do you have cute stationery in your drawer somewhere? Pull it out today.

Letter writing counters stress. In a Kent State study, participants who wrote letters to express authentic thoughts and heartfelt gratitude experienced an increase in overall happiness. Research shows that writing letters to express your love activates parts of the brain that releases happy hormones like endorphin and dopamine. Depressive symptoms decreased significantly.

When you recall a friend or loved one's voice and touch, your body actually reexperiences how you feel when you're with that person. Loved.

Better

Only one thing is needed.
Let my love renew you today.

Only *one thing is needed.*
You don't need to be or do better
—just *loved better.*

Hear Jesus whisper:
Don't worry. Just let me love you.
Hold my hand. Just rest.

"Your love, oh Lord, reaches to the heavens. Your
faithfulness stretches to the skies." PSALM 36:5

"Most of the things we need in order to be most fully alive never come from busyness. They grow out of rest."

MARK BUCHANAN

I woke up this morning, my heart stilted in a fog, overthinking an impending decision. So I drove out to the ocean.

As each wave tumbled onto the sand like blossoms blown across a meadow, God's reassuring peace and love washed over my troubled soul—and it somehow became clear to me, as I walked and watched the cleansing tide smooth the wet shore:

Don't choose the step that you think will lead you to more clarity.
Don't think about who would love you more for which choice.
Choose what God has quietly whispered into your heart.

Small and fragile, but beautiful to you. Maybe only you.
Be the little girl who holds only one thing in her hand: God's hand.
Be the Beloved.

My soul exhaled and I smiled again, as the sun sparkled in my heart once more.

Walking by faith is the harder choice, but it's the only choice to feel alive again. Choosing to nurture your heart gives God space to renew your joy each day.

READ GOD'S STORY

When our hearts becomes gripped with what-if scenarios, complicated options, and uncertainty, Jesus brings to mind words he once whispered to someone like us. Jesus came to spend time with Martha and her sister, Mary, when Martha felt all alone, overwhelmed with the details of creating a perfect visit for him.

Listen to Jesus share his heart with you now. But hear him speak truth *in a gentle voice, a voice of Someone who is never critical but instead cares about your troubles deeply* and *who calls you Beloved.*

Imagine the intimacy Martha shared with Jesus, when she confided in him, unguarded, as friends, straight from her heart in turmoil.

> Martha had a sister called Mary who sat at the Lord's feet listening to what he said. But Martha was distracted by all the preparations that had to be made.
>
> She came to Jesus and asked, "Lord, do you not care that my sister has left me alone to serve?"
>
> The Lord said to her, "Martha, Martha, you are worried and troubled about so many things.
> But only one thing is necessary. Mary has chosen what is better."
>
> LUKE 10:39–42

Jesus wanted something deeper. *Better.* He wanted Martha to be loved. Jesus didn't love Martha for what she could do for him. He wanted her to receive everything he longed to give her—*himself.* Jesus wanted to hold her and bring her soul peace with his whispers of rest.

Stop. Slow. Listen.

Jesus whispers this same invitation to you today:

Just one thing is needed. Choose to be my Beloved.

Let God renew you with His love once again.

A New You

Sometimes, even when we know the truth, we still worry. Jesus understands. Those are times we can put our worries in

Jesus' hands—and take a break from our worries—to free ourselves to rest and refresh. That was what Jesus was telling Martha to do—to put the worry of the visit into God's hands, so
she could be free to just sit, relax, and enjoy his company.

What is *one thing* you can do today that brings you pleasure—
that helps you to slow down and relax—as a way to enjoy the
presence of God's peace and joy? Take just one step closer to
hearing God's whisper of rest on your heart today.

Like Martha, we may prefer to work rather than feel. It feels
less vulnerable than receiving and nurturing our spirit. Maybe
we prefer to earn our moments of peace and joy, so that no one
can accuse us of not deserving it. Maybe we've been taught
that it's safer to *do* for others, rather than relaxing and enjoying
something that feeds our soul. Somehow, we've carried that
self-deprivation mind-set into how we relate to God.

*Jesus sees the inner you who has wants and needs, even if the outer
you is used to protecting herself by doing.* Jesus wants you to choose
what's better—to lay down what everyone else expects of you
and free your heart to be his.

God is making all things new—in you. Don't wait until
your life is work free or problem free before spending time on
what really matters—love, relationships, and nurturing your
inner spirit. Let Jesus hold you and your worries all together—
so *you can take a break and choose what's better.* Feeding your soul.
Rest.

Refresh yourself in the *unique* way that speaks to *your* personality and interests with Jesus. Then, you will return with
your spirit reenergized, able to move as God inspires you, and
tackle your worries, which will feel a whole lot smaller.

Step out. Be the renewed you. Be loved.

ℐ God's Whispers to You

Beloved,
You only need to choose one thing.
Not to be better—but loved better.

You only need to be loved.

Come close. Listen to whatever I whisper to you.
Choose to be my Beloved.
Hold on to me. Let my love renew you today.
Just rest.

ℐ A Prayer for Today: When You're Worried

"Your love, oh Lord, reaches to the heavens.
Your faithfulness stretches to the sky."   PSALM 36:5

Dear Jesus,
Your love reaches to the heavens.
Now, help me to reach for your hand.

I'm worried about too many things.

Give me the courage to lay down the roles and responsibilities
you never intended me to own.

Give me courage to choose what's better for me today—
to simply rest.

I choose to be your little girl,
holding nothing but your hand today.
I choose you.
Amen.

Give Yourself Permission: Take one thing off of your list today that drains you. Free up space to do the one thing that revitalizes you and gives you pleasure.

REFLECT ON YOUR STORY

1. *What is distracting or worrying you?*

2. *What is one thing you can do to take off your list today that drains you? And what is one thing you can do that energizes you?*

3. *How is the One Word BETTER speaking to you today?*

PRAY & REST

A SIMPLE PRACTICE: SONG MEDITATION

Jesus invites us to experience what is so much *better*: resting in him. Brother Lawrence, a seventeenth-century Carmelite monk and author of *The Practice of the Presence of God*, pioneered a new concept of prayer and spiritual intimacy and work in his monastery. He intentionally paused to talk with God anywhere, any time, and in any way—even while washing dishes: "There is not in the world a kind of life more sweet and delightful, than that of a continual conversation with *God*: those only can comprehend it who practice and experience it."

One simple way to intentionally enjoy *continual conversation* with God as Brother Lawrence did is by listening to songs. *A song is a quiet conversation* echoed in music. For today's prayer, listen to a worship song that speaks to you. *Write the song lyrics as a prayer prompt. Reflect on the One Word Prayer* BETTER.

TODAY'S BELOVED CHALLENGE

Listen To Your Favorite Worship Song

Pick two songs to enjoy as you walk or relax in the sun, or before you sleep tonight.

Take ten minutes. Make music your time of meditation and prayer. Find new songs or load favorites into your playlist. Let God renew you through song today.

SOUL CARE TRAIL NOTES

Music Is Therapy for the Soul

As an experiment, Brother Lawrence made it *a habit to intentionally think of God* during the day. "I worshipped Him as often as I could, keeping my mind in His holy presence, and *recalling it* as often as I found I had *wandered* from Him."

Songs give us a simple way to practice the presence of God—to recall us back to Him during the day. Music is also used in therapy to uncover hidden emotional responses in children, helping them find words to express themselves. Songs give them permission to examine what's bothering them or to process their experiences.

Music therapy is not just for children. Music helps us pray without words. Music is shown to bring calm and comfort, and alleviate pain. When you feel too stressed to pray, put on some music and let God whisper words of rest and love to you.

Delight

You are named. You are my Delight.

Under the rubble of broken dreams,
I cherish what no one sees. You belong to me.

You don't have to do or say something special.
You don't have to earn my love.
You are named. You are my Delight.
My love is here to stay.

*"But you will be named my Delight... For the Lord
delights in you."* ISAIAH 62:4

"And now, with God's help, I shall become myself."

SØREN KIERKEGAARD

I once asked my mother why she chose my name.

She was just seventeen when I was born in San Francisco's Chinatown. Newly emigrated from Hong Kong, my mother hadn't learned English yet. The nurse read to her from a book of names, and when she heard *Bonnie*, she found it easy to pronounce and simple to holler out. And that was how I got my name.

Sometimes, I'd try to remember how my father said my name. Funny thing is, we often remember someone's voice, depending on how we last heard it—like a needle, etching a groove on a record, laying down tracks. For seven-year-old me, watching her daddy drive off with his bags packed in his Nova, the last time he said my name, he said good-bye.

It's significant how you are named. It's important who says your name and how they say it. *It matters who you belong to.*

Do you remember when someone whispered your name with love in the night—a voice who told you: *You are loved?*

Were you in pj's as Grandma or Mom hushed your cough away, rubbing Mentholatum into your skin? Was it your father hugging you to calm a bad dream? Or was it your husband drawing you to himself that first night, on the day he vowed to be yours until death do you part?

God Whispers Your Name

Before you could remember, God breathed His very self into you, gently tracing His fingerprints onto your hand, planting His dreams into yours. It was your Heavenly Father naming you *Beloved* with His whispers. As time passed, God collected your tears in a bottle, bringing the river to melt the snow into spring, so that now you can see beauty, even when it rains.

It may be hard to remember our name when critical voices confuse us. One step into the noise of Facebook, we suddenly feel lost. Studies show people get depressed from merely viewing updates on social media. Pulses quicken. Blood pressures rise. Our brains are wired to compare disparate objects. So we end up objectifying *what we have* or *what we do*—rather than *who we are*.

We compare ourselves with who we were in the past (voices of regret), who we could be in the future (voices of perfectionism), or should have been (voices of shame). The world labels us, but God knows our true name.

How are you allowing the world—your past, how you look, what you own, who you know, your failures, or successes—to name you?

Names are so significant, God renamed a lot of people.

Jacob to Israel. After a night of wrestling wounded, Jacob's name changed from *to trip up* to *God endures.* (Genesis 32:24–28)

Saul into Paul. Paul's name changed from *demanded* to *small* after his baptism. (Acts 13)

Simon to Peter. Peter was renamed from *being his father's son* to *how Jesus saw him*: the rock. (John 1:42)

The significance of your names lies in *who* calls your name. *Could God be renaming you?*

READ GOD'S STORY

Put aside the other voices crowding in. Listen as God renames you:

"You will no longer be called 'Forsaken'...
But you will be named my Delight...
For the Lord delights in you."   ISAIAH 62:4–5

Imagine God rejoicing over you. Does it feel awkward to accept this name: *my Delight?* It's vulnerable to believe something so audacious that says: *You don't have to earn my love. You are my delight. As is.*

The world says the opposite: Keep doing whatever it takes to be loved and then you'll be worthy of love. Not only that, the world says we need to *continually* earn our worth, in order to be accepted, included, noticed, valued, or given opportunity to belong or succeed. The minute we make a mistake or fail to meet someone's expectations of being special, beautiful, smart or "good enough," we have to perform and start all over again.

It's an exhausting treadmill of striving in our jobs, friendships, family standing, ministry, or social circles. We've learned that *love can be lost,* because whoever might have given us love holds the power to take it away.

Our worth becomes tied to *what we do for others,* but God announces a stunning truth: Your worth is tied to *what God does for you.* He loves you. God chooses you *continually.*

And the mind-boggling twist is that God finds us utterly captivating and valuable, in the very moments we are doing absolutely zilch or completely failing in every way. God pursues us because loving us—*seeing us come alive when we receive His love in our most imperfect moments*—brings Him joy. We are His Beloved.

God reassures us that His love is different. *His love is unconditional.* It lasts.

"His love endures forever."   PSALM 136:1

✐ God's Whispers to You

Hear God tenderly whisper to you now:

Beloved,
Under the rubble of broken dreams,
I cherish what no one sees. You belong to me.

You don't have to do or say anything special.
You don't have to earn my love. I freely give it.

You are named. You are my Delight.
My love is here to stay.

Whatever this day holds, move in the direction as God prompts you. You are loved. You are named.

✐ A Prayer for Today: When God Whispers Your Name

"But you will be named my Delight…
For the Lord delights in you."   ISAIAH 62:4–5

Dear Jesus,
I could hold on and stay safe here
behind all the voices that push me to do and be more.
But I want to rest in the name you give me.

Give me courage to move out, to speak, to act,
to love, to dream, and to make choices today
as someone who is beloved.
Speak into this heart of mine. Change me deep as I step out.

Help me say yes to what aligns with your name for me: my
DELIGHT.
And say no to what doesn't. Today.
Amen.

One day we'll stand before Jesus and look into his eyes, as he hands us a white smooth stone, forever etched with our true names. You'll hear his voice, calling you *Beloved*, announcing your name.

"To him who overcomes… I will give him a white stone and a new name written on the stone."

REVELATIONS 2:17

Give Yourself Permission: Set aside time to enjoy something that uses your natural interests, gifts, and strengths. Be bold. Choose what matches your personality, energizes your spirit, and explores your gifting. Let go of what doesn't.

REFLECT ON YOUR STORY

1. *What names or labels have others put on you? What do you say about yourself?*

2. *How do you feel when God calls you "my Delight"? What changes would you make, if you really believed it?*

3. *What One Word speaks to you today?*

PRAY & REST

A SIMPLE PRACTICE: GOD'S LOVE LETTER TO YOU

Søren Kierkegaard, a Danish theologian and philosopher, wrote about experiencing Christ through our *emotions as individuals responding to God's love.* "The function of prayer is not to influence God, but rather to change the nature of the one who prays." How is God's love changing your nature?

Today's One Word Prayer is *DELIGHT.* Take a moment now to be still. As you enter into prayer, sit relaxed. Hear God whisper His name for you: *my Delight.*

If Jesus wrote you a letter—*to share a list of what he delights about you*—what would he say? Give Jesus a chance to speak as your pen flows on the page.

Dear _____ (your name),

What I love about you is the way you... (your personality)

The things you value... (your inner beauty)

How you get lost enjoying... (your interests)

Because I created you with love, my heart feels delight—when I see you energized, exercising your strengths... (your gifts and talents)

TODAY'S BELOVED CHALLENGE

Write a Self-Affirmation Sticky Note
"I am ___"
Place it where you can see it.

When something happens today and you realize—*I did that well, or I liked how I handled that*—write it down. Let your sticky note be a reminder of God's love note to you. *You are my Delight.*

SOUL CARE TRAIL NOTES

Self-Affirmations Make a Difference

We all know that simply saying, "I'm fine," doesn't help us. God wants us to be honest. But did you know that agreeing with how God sees us—when we tell ourselves the truth about our *values and strengths*—replenishes the spark in us?

Research shows that *when people spontaneously reflect on their strengths* during the day—even when they're chronically stressed to begin with—their self-affirmations offset the negative effects of stress and act as a buffer. People experience a boost in energy and creativity, solving problems more easily than those who didn't say them. Studies show you can feel more hopeful, happier, and optimistic, and less sad and angry, by writing down your strengths and what is important to you.

ᗡ ᗡ ᗡ

Beloved

You are cherished. You are my Beloved.

There is no place that we can go,
where God's love for us cannot go deeper.

In His quiet embrace,
we don't have to do more or be more.

Jesus whispers,
You are cherished. You are my Beloved.

"You are my Beloved… In you, I take delight." MARK 1:11

Many voices ask for our attention..."Prove that you are a good person."..."You'd better be ashamed of yourself."..."Nobody really cares about you," and one that says, "Be sure to become successful, popular and powerful." But underneath all these often very noisy voices is a still, small voice that says, "You are my Beloved, my favor rests on you."

That's what prayer is. It is listening to the voice that calls us "my Beloved."   HENRI NOUWEN

Sometimes I start the day with the best of intentions.

I figure out a game plan: people to talk to, decisions to make, and things to do. I feel in control. But as the day unfolds, I am often overwhelmed.

The world pressures me to make things happen. Now. But when things don't go as planned, I often try to regain control—by shutting down my heart.

That was what happened when I first started dating Eric, my husband now. I was a thirty-something single. Having kissed too many frogs, telling my story too many times over way too many coffee dates, yet still not finding "the one," I figured I had the gift of singleness.

So when Eric and I unexpectedly started dating, I didn't think it would last. One weekend, we took a road trip to Southern California with friends to ride the crazy roller coasters at Magic Mountain.

This will be it, I thought. *Six hours alone in the car with Bonnie? This guy's finally going to figure out what he's gotten himself into.*

The day before we left, sure enough, some dysfunctional family dynamics between my mother and me came to a head, erupting in a painful argument. My heart, initially excited and hopeful, suddenly felt clouded with emotional turmoil and discouragement. But I did what I always do. I put it aside.

On the drive down, Eric and I talked music, college days, our favorite this and pet-peeve that. But I avoided the topic of family for hours. Suddenly, Eric asked about my family. Waterworks. Big time. My mascara was running.

"I'm not the girl you probably think I am," I said, deciding to pop his bubble. "My life is complicated. You don't want to get involved with me. Find someone with a more normal life."

Eric was quiet for a minute. He reached for my hand. "I don't want normal. I'm interested in you. What is it?"

As I confided, a secret tumbled out that I'd thought would drive him away. But he stayed. I tried to shut down my heart. I couldn't see the seed God had planted in my broken story. *I didn't believe that I could be flawed and yet still loved.* But Eric listened. He stayed.

God extends this same invitation to us—to be His Beloved. As we are.

God's Mission Field

Today, you may feel overwhelmed by all you have to navigate to fulfill what you view as your mission or purpose. You may feel the pressure to keep everything unbroken, by hiding your heart. To keep everything together.

But God's mission field isn't found in what you can do for Him. How your heart is doing is important to God. *Your heart is God's mission field.*

Could God be inviting you to let go of a goal, burden, or mission you're carrying today—and let Him love you instead?

READ GOD'S STORY

Listen as our Heavenly Father whispers to you, what He once said to Jesus:

"You are my Beloved…In you, I take delight."   MARK 1:11

Before Jesus performed a single miracle, he was already beloved. Jesus brought pleasure to the Father by letting go of control (see Philippians 2:17). Jesus was willing to be viewed as flawed, even though he was perfect.

Jesus didn't shut down his heart. He opened his heart to love and brokenness, so that he could one day make your heart his home. Your story is his story.

So when the day runs off the rails and you doubt your worth, lean into Jesus. Let his love fill you with courage to face whatever is in front of you. Even if things fall apart, you'll fall right into God's embrace.

The world saw nothing special about Jesus—no credentials like the thought leaders in his day—but our Heavenly Father cherished Jesus, just as He cherishes you today.

God's Whispers to You

Beloved,
I see you.
In my eyes, you are everything
I've always dreamed you would be.

Others might see you as unfinished.
But you are perfectly complete in me.
My love makes you whole.

You are cherished.
You are my Beloved.
In you, I am well pleased.

Just as the sun rises in the east and sets in the west, you rest at the very center of God's pleasure—simply because you are His.

✍ *A Prayer for Today:*
Listen to the Voice Calling You Beloved

"You are my Beloved...In you, I take delight." MARK 1:11

Dear Heavenly Father,
Help me let go when my plans don't line up
with what I want them to be today.

And when I feel things are falling out of control,
give me courage to follow your lead ahead
because you see beyond my flaws
and you call me Beloved.

Let your gentle voice be my guide today.
Let the pleasure of your love set me free.
Thank you for loving me.
Amen.

Whatever happens today, let go of your plans and hold on to God's hand instead. *You are cherished.* You are beloved.

Give Yourself Permission: Listen to your heart. Rest and refresh yourself, or connect with people and conversations, instead of getting more done. Hold your plans loosely. Your well-being is more important. What's urgent to others doesn't have to be urgent to you.

REFLECT ON YOUR STORY

1. *What are two things you would take off your plate if someone gave you permission to let them go?*

2. *Think back. Describe a moment in your life when you felt beloved.*

3. *What does it mean to you—to be "beloved" today?*

4. *What One Word speaks to you today?*

PRAY & REST

A SIMPLE PRACTICE: MORNING PRAYERS

Before the day begins, pray a *Morning Prayer*. It's a way for you to invite Jesus to step into the day ahead with you—to share your feelings and schedule with him. Focus on the events that you're excited about and the ones that hold uncertainty or cause you stress.

Today's One Word Prayer is *BELOVED*. Close your eyes and imagine that *you and Jesus are walking through each hour together*—looking at the places you'll go, people you'll see, conversations you'll have, or decisions you'll need to make. Pause at each one and ask Jesus for whatever you need: encouragement, peace, strength, or wisdom. He'll meet you in a very real way as you face them together.

Jesus, here is what I feel most excited about or desire for today . . .

Here is what I feel most hesitant or stressed about today . . .

TODAY'S BELOVED CHALLENGE

Enjoy a Cup of Coffee or Tea

Coffee brightens your mood. Tea brings calm.
Take a break, sip, and rest.

What's your favorite coffee drink or tea? Enjoy it with Jesus.

SOUL CARE TRAIL NOTES

Drinking Coffee or Tea Is Good For Your Soul

John Baille, a Scottish theologian in the 1900s, expressed his Morning Prayers in *A Diary of Private Prayer*: "Eternal Father of my soul, let my first thought today be of you…From moments of quietness, let light…remain with me through all hours of the day."

During the day, take breaks to return to the peace of your morning prayer. Enjoy a cup of tea—a cup of quietness. I share tea with friends, and at night I brew a pot of tea for Eric and me to unwind and talk about the day together.

Studies show that even the ritual of making tea, by placing a kettle on the stove, releases a calming response associated with memories of enjoying tea. Scientists have found that drinking a single cup of tea reduces anxiety levels by up to 25 percent in participants after they've experienced a stressful moment.

As for coffee, a Harvard study shows that coffee brightens your mood, helps fight depression, and lowers the risk of suicide. Caffeine stimulates the central nervous system and boosts production of neurotransmitters like serotonin, dopamine, and noradrenaline, which elevate your mood. Two cups of coffee a day can prevent the risk of suicide by 50 percent.

And if you don't want the caffeine and prefer decaf, *just smelling coffee* can make you less stressed! Research found that inhaling the aroma of coffee changed brain proteins connected to stress. Coffee can make you feel happier, because it is rich in antioxidants, which researchers attribute to coffee's mood-lifting benefits.

PART TWO

Choosing as the Beloved

Reclaim Your Self-Worth

As you embrace your identity as God's Beloved,
you will start valuing yourself the way God does.

Hear God whisper—
You are worth it. Just rest.

This next set of devotionals welcomes you
*to reclaim your self-worth
and choose every good and perfect gift—*
cascading from your Heavenly Father's heart
to lovingly bless you each day.

*"Every good and perfect gift is from above,
coming down from the Father of the heavenly lights."*

JAMES 1:17

Choose Joy

You are worth it. Joy is meant for you.

In your quiet moments,
you may wonder if joy is worth choosing—
whether *you* are worth prioritizing.

Jesus hears your unspoken longing for joy.
Jesus replies—
You are worth it.
Joy is meant for you.

*"These things I have spoken to you so that my joy may
be in you, and that your joy may be made full."*

JOHN 15:11

> "May what I do flow from me like a river, no forcing and
> no holding back, the way it is with children."
>
> RAINER MARIA RILKE

I'm a night owl. When the house is quiet and the moon is still,
I start waking up. This wasn't always true. I once loved getting
up in the morning.

In high school, extracurricular classes like orchestra began
at 7:00 a.m., before the morning bell. I lived far from school,
on the other side of the railroad tracks. So I'd wake up at 5:30
a.m. and take public transportation Bus No. 55.

The bus would lurch to a squeaky stop, the wobbly back
doors would swing open, and I'd sleepily disembark in front
of Fremont High. Walking through the empty hallways to
the school auditorium at dawn felt peaceful. I can still hear the
click of my violin case, opened once I'd settled myself into my
chair on the stage. The room would be dark except for the
spotlights shining on us as we practiced.

There is something utterly beautiful and simple—so quietly alluring—about getting lost doing something you enjoy.
My violin was a loaner from the school, and I never had private lessons. But I loved the sound of the bow gliding across
the strings, playing in unison with others moved by the same
music.

I didn't have to be good at it. But for one magical hour of
the day, time flew by. *I was happy. Playing the violin gave me joy.*

Looking back now, I can see that it was God who put the
joy of music in my heart. Yet the option to choose it was left in
my hands.

The Gift of Joy

Today, God invites you to quietly lay down the things we do out of performance and busyness and instead open the gift he's placed in each of us: joy.

When did you hear music sing in your soul as a little girl?

Did it happen when you rode your bike, dipped your brush in paint, or wrote in your journal? Or did you feel joy when your hair flew as you danced, when your fingers touched the keys at your piano, or when you sang in front of the mirror with your hairbrush?

Did you spend hours creating a world for your Barbie dolls, laughing on the swings with a friend, dusting your hands in flour baking with Grandma, fishing with Grandpa—or simply reading a book while lying on your bed?

Maybe like me, you don't have a lot of childhood memories spent getting lost in joy—*but you secretly long to explore what would give you joy now.* But maybe you find it hard to prioritize joy and take time for yourself—to enjoy something that gives you pleasure. You may feel hesitant to commit time, money, or resources to choosing joy, because you're afraid if it isn't something you can market, become an expert at, or somehow help others with, it would be a waste.

Joy may *feel* selfish, but it isn't. Joy becomes your heart's response to God when you reclaim your rightful place in this world, as someone valued, seen, and important: His beloved child.

Joy challenges you to ask yourself *whether you believe you are worth prioritizing.* The truth is, a well-loved woman who chooses joy will naturally bless others, like a river being filled by refreshing spring rain.

READ GOD'S STORY

Listen to Jesus tenderly reassure the child in you to prioritize joy. Picture the little girl in you, standing in front of Jesus, as he whispers:

> "Don't push *these children away.*
> *These children [the child in you]*
> *are at* **the very center of life in God** *in the kingdom.*
>
> *Anyone who becomes as humble* **as this little child**
> *is the greatest in the kingdom of heaven.*
>
> *And anyone who welcomes a little child like this*
> *on my behalf* **is welcoming me**."
>
> MARK 10:14–16, MATTHEW 18:4, 9:37

Don't push the child in you away. Jesus' words tell us we are greatest in God's kingdom—that we best experience God's presence—*when we give ourselves permission to be like a child, who vulnerably chooses joy with Jesus.*

When you make time to choose joy as God's little girl—to be His beloved daughter—*you begin to welcome spending time with Jesus.* These are soul-changing words. They redefine the importance of prioritizing joy.

Joy is spiritual intimacy with God.

✐ God's Whispers to You

Dear Beloved Daughter,
Tell me what brings you joy.
Welcome me in your arms. Say yes.

You are worth it. Joy was meant for you.
Choose joy. With me. Today.

Choosing to perform for others may seem easier. But joy is radical vulnerability of the soul that dares say, "I am God's Beloved and I will rest in Him."

✍ *A Prayer for Today:* *Dare to Choose Joy*

"These things I have spoken to you so that my joy may be in you, and that your joy may be made full."

JOHN 15:11

Dear Jesus,
Thank you for simple joys—
gifts you've given to me.

No matter how much time has passed,
the little girl in me who feels joy
is still safe with you.

Revive that part in me now.
Breathe your Holy Spirit into me and fan the flames.
Give me courage to choose joy.
With you. Today.
Amen.

Give Yourself Permission: Put aside whatever keeps you from being a child with Jesus today. Choose the little things that give you joy. Be God's Beloved.

REFLECT ON YOUR STORY

1. *What have you enjoyed getting lost in doing, that once gave you joy? Why did you stop?*

2. *Share ideas about how you can choose joy today. Or begin again.*

3. *What One Word in today's Scripture speaks to you?*

PRAY & REST

A SIMPLE PRACTICE: LITTLE GIRL MOSAIC

Welcome the little girl in you to be present with Jesus now. For today's One World *JOY*, fill out...this prayer prompt—*What Brings Me Joy*—by sketching a mosaic of what brought you joy as a little girl. See Jesus light up watching you get lost in joy. He invites you to enjoy those joys again.

1. Draw a picture of yourself as a little girl in the middle of the page below.
2. Write around her, like petals on a flower, a list of things you once enjoyed:

   favorite places   *things she collected*   *music*   *foods*
   favorite activities   *people she enjoyed*   *colors*   *experiences*

TODAY'S BELOVED CHALLENGE

Do One Thing That Brings You Joy
Welcome Jesus into your day.

Choose joy as an act of faith today and God will meet you in that movement. *Joy is meant for you.*

SOUL CARE TRAIL NOTES

Sharing Your Joy Multiplies into More Joy

Henri Nouwen was a Dutch theologian and professor at Harvard Divinity School who gave up his life of prestige to care for the mentally and physically handicapped. Living among adults who expressed joy freely like children, Nouwen never felt as loved. "Joy does not simply happen to us. We have to choose joy and keep choosing it every day."

A Brigham Young University study shows that sharing positive experiences leads to heightened well-being, increased overall life satisfaction, and even more energy. Research confirms that when you share what gives you joy, that joyful feeling increases and lasts longer.

The *Little Girl Joy Mosaic* is one of the most powerful activities women experience together in the *Spiritual Whitespace Retreats* that I lead. Women come alive when they share their stories and explore how to choose joy again.

Take time today or this week to show your *Little Girl Mosaic* to a friend. Share your memories of joy and experience more joy. Ask about hers.

Choose Rest

You are loved. Choose rest.

When you're too stressed to pray,
Jesus whispers—
Lean in. To me.

You don't have to be strong.
You are loved. You are worth it.
Choose rest.

"Let the beloved of the Lord rest secure in him, for he shields him all day long, and the one the Lord loves rests between his shoulders." DEUTERONOMY 33:12

❦ ❦ ❦

"We do not believe in ourselves until someone reveals that deep inside us is something valuable, worth listening to, worthy of our trust, sacred to our touch."

ATTRIBUTED TO E. E. CUMMINGS

Sometimes you run out of words. You don't feel like praying, and God feels far away. Even though you know you ought to pray, the act feels like another box to check, which leaves you feeling guilty. Life is complicated. In an age of information a Google search away, with friends on Facebook posting photos and updates—*we can forget real life is an unfolding journey without easy answers.*

We look at our everyday lives overwhelmed with dilemmas and conflicting desires, and we get discouraged. We feel soul stressed. Ironically, when we're most stressed, we often deprive ourselves of what we need most: God's goodness.

We often burn ourselves out trying to serve God, rather than taking care of ourselves—the way God would want, if He were here in person today. Somehow, we've learned we don't deserve rest—until we've solved our problems or we're no longer struggling. It's the opposite.

What we need is God's TLC—His tender, loving care. TLC is what God gave Elijah to resuscitate his soul after his spirit was broken. We need to choose rest.

READ GOD'S STORY

Even though Elijah did everything he knew to do—even defeating the prophets of Baal—his problems did not go away. Stress broke Elijah's spirit. Listen to his whispers:

"It is enough; now, Lord, take my life,
for I am no better than my fathers."   1 KINGS 19:4

So Elijah ran away. He didn't want to see anyone or do anything anymore. He felt demoralized and done. *Then he fell asleep.*

Yet, God did not leave him or lecture him. God didn't move on to use someone else. God loved Elijah deeper and drew him closer.

In that place of despair, Elijah woke up to find fresh bread baking on hot stones and water—that God *had left just for him.* Warm bread. Water poured into a jar. Beautiful care expressed through handmade touches.

Not only that, God sent an angel—to touch him. But Elijah was so exhausted that one touch wasn't enough. God sent the angel a second time—to touch him. Again.

So when you find it's hard to pray, don't be afraid. You're standing at the very cusp of who God longs to connect with—the real you.

Your heart needs God's intimate touch. Take the time to rest. Be His Beloved.

Arise and Eat

When we give our bodies the break it longs for, we give God a chance to whisper to us what the angel said to Elijah that day:

"Arise and eat. For the journey is too great for you."
                                              1 KINGS 19:7

He did not say, "Arise and work harder."
Arise and eat. The journey is too great. These are the whispers

Elijah needed to hear for his soul to start mending. These same words of love and compassion are meant for you as well.

✑ God's Whispers to You

Beloved,
I know you're tired. The journey is too great for you.
Tell me, Beloved. What do you need to renew your spirit?

You don't have to be strong enough.
You are loved. You are worth it.
Lean into me. Let me take care of you. Choose rest.

God invites you to stop and rest to sustain you for the journey. It was only after resting and physically unplugging that Elijah found the strength to go on—*not to return to work again, but to crawl into a cave.*

Sometimes, the bravest thing we can do is admit we are tired and discouraged. We need to physically get away and face how we really feel about things, do some soul searching, and reassess what we are doing and why we are doing them.

Far away from life as he knew it, Elijah met God up close. Not in the earthquake that shifted the ground. Not in a magnificent fire everyone could see. *God came to him in a whisper— through the kiss of a gentle breeze.*

> *"After the earthquake came a fire, but the Lord was not in the fire. And after the fire came a gentle whisper."*
> 1 KINGS 19:12

God knew Elijah needed TLC first—touch, physical rejuvenation, food, drink, sleep, and emotional safety—in order to hear His gentle voice. God's TLC rejuvenates you to feel His nearness again. Be brave. Choose to rest.

𝒟 *A Prayer for Today:*
When You Feel Too Stressed to Pray

"Let the beloved of the Lord rest secure in him, for he shields him all day long, and the one the Lord loves rests between his shoulders." DEUTERONOMY 33:12

Dear Jesus,
The journey is too great. I'm tired. I need your touch.
I have no more words. Will you take care of me?
Give me courage to receive your TLC.

Help me to be brave enough to rest.
To physically unplug, to let someone in and feel a hug,
to eat better, find emotional relief,
sleep, maybe cry, or soul-search.
Thank you for always staying with me,
loving me unconditionally.
Amen.

Give Yourself Permission: It's okay to have limits. Everyone does. Be honest if you're burned out and discouraged. Take a break from toxic relationships. Decommit from responsibilities for a season. Schedule a personal TLC soul retreat to eat well, sleep, enjoy what reenergizes you, soul-search, or simply breathe.

REFLECT ON YOUR STORY

1. *Circle which kind of TLC do you need most today? Share why.*

   Physical touch   Sleep   Eating better

   Physical Rest—space to unplug and get away

   Emotional Rest—safety to be honest and understood

   Spiritual Encouragement—Soul-searching guidance and
       direction

2. *God uses people—angels in our friends—to encourage us. How easy/difficult is it for you to make time for friends? To be vulnerable instead of capable?*

3. *What One Word in Scripture speaks to you today?*

PRAY & REST

A SIMPLE PRACTICE: PRAY USING VISUAL IMAGERY

You don't always need words to pray. For today's prayer, use visual imagery as meditation with God. Richard Foster writes in *The Celebration of Discipline*, "As with meditation, the imagination is a powerful tool in the work of prayer... Imagination often opens the door to faith." Jesus himself used visual imagery in parables to powerfully connect people to his heart.

Close your eyes. Picture yourself in a situation or facing a decision, like watching a scene in a movie. Invite Jesus to stand beside you, as you replay those scenes. *How does Jesus respond to what's happening—what does he say or do—as you both watch these scenes unfold? Write your prayer using today's One Word Prayer, REST, here:*

— 🍃 🍃 🍃 —

TODAY'S BELOVED CHALLENGE
Give Yourself Some TLC
Choose one:

- Cook yourself (or treat yourself to) a warm meal.
- Savor your favorite coffee drink or tea.
- Nourish your body with a nap, a bath, or quiet reading.
- Get in "touch" with a big hug for a friend, spouse, or child.

God loves seeing you at rest. *You're worth it. Choose rest.*

SOUL CARE TRAIL NOTES

The Importance of Comfort

When you are too stressed to pray, take care of yourself. Richard Swenson in *The Overload Syndrome* writes, "Chronic overloading is not a spiritual prerequisite for authentic Christianity...We can learn a lesson from Jesus—it's okay to have limits. It is okay not to be all things to all people all of the time all by ourselves."

Extend yourself the kindness and comfort you generously give others. Ironically, the times we most need God's comfort are times we deprive ourselves of care. We may feel selfish. *Yet, God says we can comfort others only with the comfort we first receive ourselves* (see 2 Corinthians 1:4). Instead of layering on guilt, let God love you through your choices to prioritize taking care of you!

Choose Quiet Love

Don't worry about tomorrow.
Let me love you today.

When you come to a fork in the road today—
between *choosing the quiet* or *filling it up,*
by performing, pleasing, or disappearing—stop.

Choose what's harder but more soul filling.
Enjoy something no one would be able to point at
and say, "Look. She did something."

Choose instead *to be loved.*
Let God love you.
Choose quiet love.

"The Lord is with you. He will take great delight in you;
He will quiet you with his love."   ZEPHANIAH 3:17

> "The world today is hungry not only for bread but hungry for love...But you cannot give what you don't have. That's why it is necessary to deepen your life of prayer. Allow Jesus...to pray with you and through you."
>
> MOTHER TERESA OF CALCUTTA

Something big is changing in me. It's as quiet as it feels beautiful and odd. Because I've always been a planner, I like to plot my steps by where I want to go—and then I figure out how to get there. That is how my todays have been planned. *To get to a destination.*

But God is longing to be more than a destination. *He's offering me His hand instead of a map.* God is inviting me to a new way of living—and I believe this invitation is for you, too.

God is calling us: *Let my quiet love bring you peace. Today.*

A quieter Voice is calling us to stop—stop worrying and planning for tomorrow as a way of distraction—and listen to what He has to say to us *today.* This Voice is kinder. More loving than the voices that push us, rush us, and criticize us, this Voice provides just what we need this very moment. To trust Him beyond what we can't see ahead.

This Voice is Jesus calling—*You were made for more. Be my Beloved. Rest in quietness. Today.*

This is hard, because we are used to providing for ourselves. It's how we've been conditioned in this world. Being busy instead of beloved. But even among our doubts, Jesus' gentle voice reassures us that being loved is the better way.

READ GOD'S STORY

Draw close as Jesus calls us to choose his quiet love in Matthew 6:26–29:

Do not worry about tomorrow.

Look at the wildflowers,
they do not toil.
Yet how beautifully I've made them.

Look at the birds,
they do not till or store,
Yet I feed and care for them.
How much more you mean to me—than any of these?

Are you worried that what you need won't show up when you need it? Are you looking for acceptance from others or a greater self-acceptance?

Jesus understands our self-doubt. Like daily manna, he gives us what we need, but only for today. No more. No less. Just enough.

Look into your heart. Take the provision and the inspiration, wisdom, or idea—*that is just enough for one step today.*

Choose the quiet, and as you do, you'll be rejuvenated with something beautiful: God's presence. *You return to being God's precious child—worthy of His undivided attention, kindness, and gentle love.* Your name is on God's heart, and your challenges and disappointments are always on His mind. Like a star twinkling in the night, God tenderly promises to take care of you.

"Can a woman forget her nursing child?
… Though she may forget, I will not forget you.
I have inscribed you on the palms of my hands;
your walls are continually before me."   ISAIAH 49:15–16

Quiet Is Intimacy

Like a window that opens the soul, quiet is our invitation to welcome God into our today. *Quiet puts everything else on hold for a moment so that you can be held by God's calm and peace.*

Quiet is intimacy where God whispers, "I'm here. For you."

> *"The Lord is in your midst. He will take great delight in you. He renews [quiets] you with his love."* ZEPHANIAH 3:17

We were made to crave peace and tranquility. To feel the sun on a walk, relish a book, plant flowers in a garden, or create art in quietness. Nothing makes a woman more beautiful than the inner glow of love. God's love renews your soul in the quiet.

Quiet can be brief or long. *Just intentional.* Quiet isn't the absence of movement. Quiet is a *movement to trust* you were meant for more than striving. You were meant to be fully alive. *When you give yourself permission to just breathe, you can just be.*

In turn, quietness brings *what really matters into focus* and *propel you* toward rest and activity that is meaningful, authentic to your true self, and energizing to your soul.

In quietness, we realize:

We *need* to feel God's touch,
We *miss* the voice of a friend,
We're *moved* to pick up our art, laugh, sing, or shed tears,
It's *time* to let go of something big,
So we can *say yes* to something small, but good for our
   soul.

We can forgive ourselves and begin anew again. *Today.*

🖋 *God's Whispers to You*

Beloved,
In quietness, you don't have to be strong. You can be loved.

You don't have to know the way ahead. I do.
Hold on to me. I'm holding on to you.

Don't be afraid.
Tomorrow will come and I will be there with you.

Like manna falling from my heart into your hands,
my words will always find their way to you.
My love will renew you. Today.

🖋 *A Prayer for Today:*
When You Need God's Quiet Love

"The Lord is with you. He will take great delight in you;
He will quiet you with his love."   ZEPHANIAH 3:17

Dear Jesus,
I don't want to distract myself
with busyness anymore.

Quiet me with your love.
Bring calm and peace to me again.

Help me let go of my worries about tomorrow
so I can be fully present today.

Instead of filling every hour
by performing, pleasing or disappearing—
I choose the quiet
to let you love me instead.

Thank you. I love you.
Amen.

Give Yourself Permission: Take *Quietness Breaks* throughout the day.

(*Outer quietness*) Unplug digitally. Turn off your phone, computer, and TV. Tune into the natural sounds of quiet. Put your phone on "Do Not Disturb" mode. Answer e-mails and other messages periodically, instead of constantly refreshing for updates.

(*Inner quietness*) Look outside, journal, or take a walk. Enjoy something creative. Make something with your hands.

REFLECT ON YOUR STORY

1. *Reflect on how much time you spend on the following activities: too much, too little, or just enough?*

    Working:

    Checking e-mail, social media:

    Being outside in nature:

    Spending time with in-real-life friends:

    Enjoying creative activities:

    Nurturing your soul or body with relaxing Me Time:

Enjoying mealtimes:
Sleep:

2. *How can you choose quiet today?*

3. *What One Word in today's beautiful Scriptures speaks to you?*

PRAY & REST

A SIMPLE PRACTICE: SILENCE AND PRAYER WALK

Mother Teresa, who daily served the poor on the noisy streets of Calcutta, tells us, "We need to find God, and he cannot be found in noise and restlessness. God is the friend of silence. See how nature—trees, flowers, grass—grows in silence; see the stars, the moon and the sun, how they move in silence. We need silence to be able to touch souls."

Practice silence for prayer today. Take a ten- to twenty-minute Prayer Walk outside. No need for spoken words. Turn off your phone. Listen to God in nature. Notice colors and movement. Feel the breeze. Walk slowly. If your mind wanders, return to the One Word phrase: *QUIET LOVE.*

"In repentance and rest you will be saved; in quietness and trust is your strength."   ISAIAH 30:15

Dear God, after spending time walking in silence with you, I feel . . .

TODAY'S BELOVED CHALLENGE

Buy Flowers for Yourself

Place them where you can enjoy them.

May the flowers remind you how valuable you are to Jesus. He is your peace.

SOUL CARE TRAIL NOTES

Flowers Improve Emotional Health

We all need encouraging reminders of peace. I love that Jesus points us *to look at flowers in the field.* Behavioral research at Rutgers University found that simply looking at flowers improves emotional health. The *presence* of flowers triggered happy emotions in participants, increasing feelings of life satisfaction. Flowers are a natural mood enhancer!

Harvard University even demonstrated that those who aren't morning people, who start out with "morning blahs," reported a *boost in energy, happiness, and friendliness that lasted throughout the day*—by looking at flowers first thing in the morning, placed in a room they frequented, particularly in the kitchen.

ᘔ ᘔ ᘔ

Choose Help

Cast your cares on me. I will help you.

Rather than stressing out
to get as much done as you possibly can today,
make the space to let God love you
as much as He possibly can.

Stop. Do what refreshes your soul.
God whispers—*Cast your cares on me.*
I will help you today.

"Cast all your cares on him because he cares for you."
1 PETER 5:7

"Prayer is taking a chance that against all odds...we are loved and chosen, and do not have to get it together before we show up."
ANNE LAMOTT

For weeks I kept myself productive. *Everything was fine. I should be thankful*, I scolded myself. But deep in my heart, where no one could see, I was troubled with worry.

Cares have a way of reappearing on our paths, don't they? As I hiked up a trail one morning, I doubled up my powers of analysis to solve a dilemma I was stuck in. I figured if I circled around my problems long enough, I'd lasso them into submission and find my way out.

But all it did was fill my mind with more pros and cons. Every time I came up with a good reason *for* one solution, I'd find another reason *against* it. This tug of war left my heart frozen in exhaustion. As I reached the top of the mountain and turned back to walk down, I wondered, *Why isn't God answering my prayers?*

Do you ever feel this way—wondering why God is silent? I felt alone. Since God couldn't be the culprit, shame filled my heart, as I concluded I must be the one failing to hear Him speak.

I don't know what to do. Help me. This was my unspoken cry.

Like Petals Opening

As I made my way down through tall grass growing unruly from the rain, I noticed something that hadn't been there on my way up. Specks of orange poppies were blossoming, opening up under the sunlight breaking through the clouds, moving shadows across the hillside.

How did I miss the poppies walking up? It turns out poppies close tight as a bud when it's cold and windy. They're so sensitive to the elements, folding in at night in the dark, you wouldn't know they were even there. Yet, when warmed by the sun in daylight, the petals open—releasing new seed to virgin soil.

Each of us is like that poppy, our petals released to open when we cast our cares into the warmth of God's hands. It may seem like He's silent. But God hears our unspoken prayers for help.

God calls us to rest in His love, just like flowers opening by sunlight in the field. We can choose to lean on God's help.

READ GOD'S STORY

When you don't know what to do, God whispers—*Cast your cares on me.*

> "Cast all *your anxiety [cares] on* him because he cares for you."   1 PETER 5:7

Do you hear Him? God will never tire. He'll say it again and again:

> "Don't be afraid, for I am with you.
> Don't be discouraged, for I am your God.
> I will strengthen you and help you.
> I will hold on to you with my right hand."   ISAIAH 41:10

When you feel like you're in the dark, with troubles battering your soul like a cold wind, Jesus sees your heart, longing to blossom by the touch of his hand.

It's the light of God's care that will set your heart free. *But you need to cast your cares on Him.* God is faithful. He is not turned off by your worries. He will not withdraw or turn aside. He's drawing you closer to Him. He cares for you.

The world teaches us that if we're troubled, we can problem-solve our way out of confusion and stress. We're trained so well in our culture to be independent. We're afraid if anyone knew we needed help, we wouldn't have anything to offer. We wouldn't be wanted.

We might live competent lives, but Jesus says—*You were made for more than this. You were made to be loved.*

God's Whispers to You

Beloved,
I see your heart, beautiful petals,
waiting to be released
from cares weighing you down.

When you don't know what to do,
I will be your daylight.

My love will strengthen you.
I will hold you. I am here for you.
Don't be afraid. Cast your cares on me.
I will help you.

Are you weary under the weight of holding everything together? Like a wildflower at rest with its petals wide open, release your anxieties to Jesus.

Jesus sees the weight of all the loose ends locked away in the quiet corners of your heart. He aches for you and longs to free you with his *complete understanding.* His loving presence will guide and help you today.

🌿 *A Prayer for Today:*
When You Don't Know What to Do

"Cast all your anxieties [cares] on him because he cares for you."   1 PETER 5:7

Dear Jesus,
Whatever is ahead of me today, you know it all.
The very thought of you taking care of me quiets my heart.
You're the one who is in control.
Guide me. Help me now.

Give me your wisdom.
Reassure me of your love.
Give me courage to do what I must do.
I cast my cares on you. Today.
Thank you, Jesus.
Amen.

Give Yourself Permission: Grieve what's hard or broken. Acknowledge that some problems can't be solved simply. Accept your limitations. Seek out and ask for help. Accept God's grace. Welcome a change of scenery and do what comforts you and brings you joy.

▨ REFLECT ON YOUR STORY ▨

1. *What cares or anxieties are you carrying?*

2. *How does it make you feel to ask for help?*

3. *What One Word speaks to you today?*

PRAY & REST

A SIMPLE PRACTICE: OPEN HANDS PETITIONING PRAYER

Today, we pray a *Petitioning Prayer* by *opening our hands, palms up*—as a vulnerable expression of faith to *request* and *receive* God's help. It reflects Philippians 4:6: "Be anxious for nothing, but in everything, by prayer and petition with thanksgiving, present your requests to God." I love how Martin Luther, founder of the Protestant Reformation, defines it: "Petitioning is stating *what we have at heart, naming the desire* we express in prayer."

Sit relaxed. Close your eyes. Open your hands. Name your request with Jesus. Rest in prayer for as long as you need. Meditate on today's One Word Prayer, *HELP.*

Dear Jesus, please help me in . . . (pour out your cares)

Think back on past times now. *Jesus, thank you for helping me when* . . .

TODAY'S BELOVED CHALLENGE

Drink Eight Cups of Water

Carry a water bottle with you and take breaks.
Staying hydrated refreshes your body and keeps stress
levels low.

Pull out a measuring cup. See how doable it is to drink the doctor-recommended eight 8-ounce glasses of water, and enjoy the break each time. Jesus is the Living Water. He will refresh you.

SOUL CARE TRAIL NOTES

Drinking Water Helps Reduce Anxiety and Depression

Even when we're too stressed to pray, Jesus helps us by praying for us. "Who is the one who condemns? No one. Christ Jesus…is also *interceding* for us" (Romans 8:34). Knowing Jesus is praying for you, prioritize your well-being.

One simple way is by drinking water. Studies show that drinking water keeps stress levels low. But not drinking enough water increases the stress hormone cortisol, inducing anxiety and stress responses—increased heart rate, nausea, fatigue, and headaches. Studies show dehydration affects our moods. When we stay hydrated, our bodies run well, leading to wellness. Water is God's natural stress reducer.

✐ ✐ ✐

Choose Comfort

Choose to be present. I will comfort you.

When you are too stressed to pray,
take care of yourself.

Hear Jesus whisper—
You can be messy.
You don't have to say anything.
Come. Let me comfort you.

Take the time. Be inconvenienced.
Choose to be present. Receive God's comfort.

"As a mother comforts her child, so will I comfort you."

ISAIAH 66:13

"The way of Jesus cannot be imposed or mapped...It's your heart, not the dictionary, that gives meaning to your words."
EUGENE PETERSON

The last time I took out my typewriter, my son Caleb was just three. Now that he's seven, he has no recollection of what the thing is. So when I got inspired to lug it out and type a few lines of poetry on it (I thought it'd look cool, retro), Caleb asked me, "What is it?"

"It's a typewriter," I answered. I told him I used it to type reports back in the '80s when I was in school. There were no computers back then.

"Where's the Delete button if you make a mistake?" Caleb asked. Before I could answer, he started banging away on it. "See?" A triplet of metal keys stuck together and ended up hammering the wrong letters onto the paper. Caleb asked if the key labeled Backspace would erase the mistake.

"No," I said, trying to recall what I used it for. "Going back doesn't fix things either. You have to start over with a fresh piece of paper. Or you get Wite-Out."

"What's Wite-Out?" But before I could explain, my little boy dressed up in his Iron Man costume, finished typing a string of mixed-up alphabets, jumped off the chair, and ran off to his next adventure.

Caleb's questions reminded me how much we try to erase the flaws in our stories—and in ourselves. We put so much pressure on ourselves to do everything right, to make everything *look* perfect: Photoshopping bodies and image-crafting perfect moments on social media. Just like that old-fashioned typewriter, we hammer away, stressed out, trying to rewrite our scripts, but get stuck instead.

This way of separating our real selves from people bleeds into our prayer lives. *We hide from God when we need Him most: when life feels flawed and we're too stressed to pray.* We withdraw from God, figuring we have little energy or optimism to offer Him.

So we end up depriving ourselves of the very thing we need that God longs to give us: His comfort. *We've forgotten that Jesus isn't looking for optimism and trouble-free prayers.* Jesus whispers:

> *When you're too stressed to pray, come to me.*
> *You can be messy. Or you don't have to say anything.*
> *Come. Let me comfort you.*

READ GOD'S STORY

Listen now as the apostle Paul encourages you, writing to believers like us:

> *"God comforts us in all our troubles*
> *so that we can comfort others.*
>
> *When they are troubled,*
> *we will be able to give them*
> *the same comfort God has given us."* 2 CORINTHIANS 1:4

Maybe God isn't offering you simple answers or new marching orders but honest-to-goodness *comfort.* Maybe we'd all stop trying to look so unflawed if we knew we weren't alone—and instead, welcomed each other with understanding, comfort, friendship and quiet listening. The very things Jesus comforts us with. Wouldn't the journey be so much more beautiful, even if it isn't perfect?

We may be very good at putting everything aside for others when we see them in need of comfort. But then we turn around and put ourselves in last place when we are in need of comfort.

Don't disappear. *Don't push away your need.* Being in touch with your need leads you to something beautiful. Jesus said, "Blessed are those who mourn, for they will be comforted" (Matthew 5:4).

Be present with how you're really feeling. God is in fact loving you right now, guiding you to revitalize your body, soul, and spirit—through the whispers of the Holy Spirit, whom Jesus calls *the Comforter.* Choose God's comfort and you'll experience His very presence!

God's Whispers to You

Beloved,
When you're too stressed to pray, come to me.
I am your Comforter.
You can be messy. Or you don't have to say anything.
Come. Let me comfort you.

Make room in your schedule.
Prioritize the comfort your soul needs.
Choose my comfort. Be my living prayer today.

We might think checking things off our to-do list will free us from stress. But it only drives us to toil and to drift farther from what truly revitalizes us: God's comfort.

A Prayer for Today:
When You Need God's Comfort

"As a mother comforts her child, so will I comfort you."
ISAIAH 66:13

Dear Jesus,
Draw near to me as I draw near to you,
just like the desert needs the rain.

I need your comfort I need your help.
Give me courage to take care of myself
the way you would,
if you were right here with me today.
Amen.

REFLECT ON YOUR STORY

1. *What are situations in which you need God's comfort?*

2. *Share an early or special memory of being comforted. What comforts you?*

3. *What is the One Word that speaks to you in today's Scripture?*

PRAY & REST

A SIMPLE PRACTICE: PRAYING THE PSALMS

Today, we comfort the soul by *Praying the Psalms*. The Psalms comfort us by speaking our heart language, when we feel dry or overwhelmed. Dietrich Bonhoeffer, theologian and martyr in *Life Together*, says, "The more deeply we grow into the Psalms...the more simple and rich will our prayer become."

Be still. Read Psalm 23:1–3 *slowly three times*:

The Lord is my shepherd, I shall not want.
He makes me lie down in green pastures;
He leads me beside quiet waters.
He restores my soul.
He guides me in the paths of righteousness for his name's sake.

Pause to meditate on each word. Circle One Word that speaks COMFORT to you. *Let a prayer, words from your heart, prompted by your One Word flow here:*

TODAY'S BELOVED CHALLENGE

Enjoy the Comfort of a Warm Bath
Pour in a bath gel or bubbles in your favorite scent.

Choose God's comfort today. You can rest. You are beloved.

SOUL CARE
TRAIL
NOTES

Taking a Bath Improves Mood and Optimism

As we prioritize God's comfort, we begin taking better care of ourselves. Because to offer others comfort, we must first receive it ourselves.

One of my favorite ways to take care of myself is ending the day with a bath, especially if it has been a stressful day. A University of Wolverhampton study found that a daily bath at the end of the day significantly improved the mood and optimism of participants, as they experienced the benefits of bodily comfort, warmth, solitude, and body positioning. Interestingly, when the body relaxes in a horizontal position in a bath, the mind associates that position with the comfort and vulnerability found in the liquid environment of the womb.

Choose Peace

I am with you. I will be your peace.

When we're tossed by life's storms,
Jesus stands close, gently whispering—
Take my hand. I will carry you through.
I am with you. I will be your peace.

"You keep him in perfect peace whose mind is stayed
on you, because he trusts in you." ISAIAH 26:3

> "Let nothing disturb you. Nothing distress you. While all
> things fade away, God is unchanging."
>
> ST. TERESA OF ÁVILA

It was my first time visiting Georgia, before the days of iPhones and instant weather reports. As I drove out to hike at a state park, the local news warned that there'd be showers on and off. But since I'd hiked in rain before, I wasn't worried.

As I parked my car at the trailhead, I realized I'd forgotten my rain gear. *Should I chance it or leave?* I had driven over an hour. I looked at the sky. The sun was shining. *I have my waterproof hiking boots on and baseball cap. I'll be fine.*

I set out to trek deep into the woods. Hours later, midpoint on the trail, it started sprinkling. Then, it poured in sheets, coming down sideways.

I found out *the weather system up on that mountain was completely different from the one back in town.* Storm clouds quickly moved in over the trees above, darkening the sky. Gusts of wind began howling. Claps of thunder rumbled to explosive booms in my ear—as lightning discharged around me in a rapid-fire fashion, like flashing strobe lights.

I was scared. Disoriented. It got so dark I couldn't see the trail well and I didn't have a flashlight. There I stood, cold and completely soaked through—in the middle of a thunderstorm—on a mountain I had never journeyed through.

Carry You Through

That's how it feels to be caught in a storm in life. Unexpected circumstances happen upon you suddenly. You feel helpless. Confused. You don't know what to do or how it will end.

Have you ever stayed up late trying to figure out a plan for peace? Are you in the middle of a storm now? Or are you watching someone you love overwhelmed by one—maybe even sinking in discouragement—and you're frightened by what it could mean?

You may feel your world spinning out of control. The truth is we aren't in control. *But God is.*

Jesus stands in the middle of our confusion and whispers, *Take my hand. I will carry you through. I am with you. I will be your peace.*

Sometimes the only way out of a dilemma is letting Jesus take you through the storm—and finding that his peace will carry you through better than any plan.

READ GOD'S STORY

Today, Jesus takes us back to a darkened storm two thousand years ago. He was alone on a mountain one night, praying for his disciples after sending them ahead into the Sea of Galilee— where they, too, met a storm. Step into this memory with Jesus.

> *"Immediately Jesus made His disciples get into the boat and go ahead of Him to the other side…*
>
> *Seeing them straining at the oars,*
> *for the wind was against them…*
> *He came to them, walking on the sea."*   MARK 6:45–48

It's hard to understand why God would send us out on a journey knowing we'd encounter a storm. But then I looked closer.

Immediately

Jesus saw them straining at the oars and he came to them. Peter attempted to walk to Jesus on water, but sank because the wind was too strong. He was afraid.

*"Immediately Jesus reached out his hand and
caught him."*   MATTHEW 14:31

Immediately, Jesus reached out his hand and lifted Peter out
of the waves.

*"But immediately Jesus spoke to them and said,
'Take heart; it is I.
Do not be afraid.'*

*Then He got into the boat with them,
and the wind stopped;
and they were utterly astonished."*   MARK 6:50-51

Jesus got into the boat with them—*immediately*. In the middle
of the storm, they no longer knew about Jesus in their heads.
They *personally experienced* Jesus in their hearts: the powerful
peace of the Master's presence.

I realize I often look for a plan to secure my peace. But God
doesn't offer us a plan. He may have a plan, but we don't get
to know it. That wouldn't require any faith. Peace is a Person.
Jesus leads us by his presence.

The only certainty we can hold on to is the Person who will
never leave us: *Jesus*. Jesus sees you straining at the oars. He will
come carry you through.

✐ *God's Whispers to You*

*Beloved,
I see the storm swirling around you,
and in you.*

Take heart. Don't be afraid.
I am faithful. I'll never leave you.

This storm isn't forever. I will get you to the other side.
Take my hand. I will carry you through.
I am with you. I will be your peace.

Jesus will take care of you. He will stay.

A Prayer for Today: For Peace in a Storm

"You keep him in perfect peace whose mind is stayed on you, because he trusts in you." ISAIAH 26:3

Dear Jesus,
Help me to see you in this storm.
Carry me back into the boat.
Calm my soul right now.

In the chaos of fear and uncertainty,
give me courage to hold on to you,
and trust this storm won't last forever.

Take my hand. Be my peace.

Thank you for being faithful. Never letting me go.
I love you.
Amen.

If you're in the middle of a journey—on your way to *the*

other side of something hard—you're not alone. We're all in the same boat *together* as disciples of Jesus.

That Rainy Day

How did my hike end? I waited for the rain to stop. But it never did, even as dusk approached. So I said a prayer and started walking downhill in the storm. I got to my car and drove back home that rainy day in Georgia. Safe and at peace.

> *"When you pass through the waters, I will be with you; and when you pass through the rivers, they will not sweep over you."* ISAIAH 43:2

Give Yourself Permission: Reassure yourself: This storm won't last forever. Prioritize bringing calm and care as God carries you through this season.

Let go of Plan A, B, or C. Take it one hour or day at a time. Reach out for help. Surround yourself with friends to support you.

▩▩ REFLECT ON YOUR STORY ▩▩

1. *What area in your life do you want more peace? What can you do or change to experience more of God's peace?*

2. *When was a time you found yourself in a storm? How did you feel?*

3. *What One Word speaks to you today?*

PRAY & REST

A SIMPLE PRACTICE: PRAYING THE NAME OF JESUS

In *The Circle of Quiet*, author Madeleine L'Engle shares, "I am slowly coming to understand with my heart as well as my head that love is not a feeling. It is a person." What brings us peace is a real person. Jesus.

For today's prayer, reflect on a name of Jesus, addressed to you.

I am *your Friend* (John 15:15)

I am *with you* (Matthew 1:23)

I am *your Light* (John 8:12)

I am *your Shepherd* (John 10:11)

I am *your Prince of Peace* (Isaiah 9:6)

I am *your Way* (John 14:6)

Today's One Word Prayer is *PEACE. Which name of Jesus brings peace to your heart now? Confide in him here...*

TODAY'S BELOVED CHALLENGE

Take a Quietness Break
Enjoy Doing Something Free of Distraction
Turn off your phone.
Take a walk in nature or savor a quiet lunch.

Love doesn't always require words. Let God touch your heart in quietness.

SOUL CARE TRAIL NOTES

Quiet Benefits the Body, Mind, and Spirit

In our modern-day efficiencies of online shopping, streaming movies, and texting, we're overloaded with information and updates. Yet the time and leisure we're supposed to gain—keys to our mental and physical health—disappears.

Quiet isn't the absence of sound. Quiet is found in ocean waves, enjoying a salad on a park bench, or walking among trees. Studies on the effects of stress show that even low-level chronic noise increases ulcers and high blood pressure. In contrast, spending time in quietness heals and restores, stimulating a mind-body connection that relaxes muscles, lowers anxiety and pain, and enhances our overall well-being.

Choose Grace

Your art, your voice matters.
Let grace in, not guilt.

Let grace in, not guilt.
Be present, not perfect.
Don't wait until the critical voices die down.

Let God's love sing over you today instead.
Your art, your voice matters. You matter.
You're worth it. Be you. Now. As is.

"Let us then approach God's throne of grace with
confidence, so that we may receive mercy and find
grace to help us in our time of need."   HEBREWS 4:16

"Real freedom is freedom from the opinion of others. Above all, freedom from your own opinions about your-self."
                                                    BRENNAN MANNING

Every day while writing my first book, *Finding Spiritual Whitespace*, the critical voice in my head said, *Who do you think you are? You think someone wants to read this? Don't waste your time.*

Maybe you hear similar voices about your own art—*about spending time or attention on something you enjoy*—a seed of God's grace planted in you. You keep checking the soil of your heart, doubting it, thinking it fell there by accident. But it's still lying quiet there, waiting for you to water it with your care and your hands.

Many times, feelings of guilt weigh us down the minute we begin to feel inspired.

You Are Worth It

It's an automatic response when I want to share something free from my heart—when I'm drawn to do something I want to enjoy. I begin to feel guilty for not doing something earlier—for something I did, didn't do, or did wrong.

I beat myself up. I replay my mistakes. I waste enormous amounts of energy reenacting how I could have done it differently. I feel bad. I feel that *I* am bad.

We become afraid to fully lean into that feeling of rest. And joy. Or peace. We might not think we deserve rest or special attention. We might not think we've earned it. We may be afraid to give time and attention to nurture our passion.

Am I really worth it? you may silently ask.

In the heart of every woman, God whispers,

Yes. You are worth it.

You are my Beloved. You are mine.

One of the reasons we allow our guilty feelings to rule is that we feel safe when we don't try. No one can hurt us if we don't do anything. We can't be rejected if we never attempt to blossom.

We won't have regrets, we tell ourselves. But there is a longing God placed in us that doesn't go away.

Every woman longs to dream, to feed her soul and rest. Everyone longs to move beyond coping and surviving. Every woman longs to be loved.

READ GOD'S STORY

Rather than driving ourselves into the ground by guilty feelings, let's see what happens when we give ourselves permission to feel inspired. *Let grace in, instead of allowing guilt to hold your heart back.*

When those critical voices start whispering, imagine Jesus standing next to you, taking your hand gently into His. Hear God's *Four Whispers of Grace* to you.

1. **Confide in God. What is He guiding you toward—or away from?**

   "It's God's kindness that leads to repentance."   ROMANS 2:4

   What words of kindness is He freeing you to fully receive today?

2. **Give attention to what refreshes your soul with God.**

   "I will send the Helper to you . . .
   When the Spirit of truth comes,
   He will guide you into all the truth."   JOHN 16:7, 13

   Enjoy the now with God today. Be present, not perfect.

3. **Discover who you are in God's eyes, rather than through the acceptance of others.**

"It is for freedom that Christ set us free.
Therefore . . . do not subject yourselves again
to the yoke of slavery."   GALATIANS 5:1

Choose to live freely, because you are beloved to your
   Heavenly Father.

4. **Make time to pursue what touches your heart, as the Holy Spirit prays for you, even in your weakness.**

"The Spirit helps our weakness . . .
The Spirit Himself intercedes for us with
groanings too deep for words."   ROMANS 8:26

Grace means we are no longer trying to make up for our
weaknesses. Give yourself permission to express God's beauty
in you—fully, just as you are.

Don't wait to be yourself with God. Not tomorrow when
you feel more qualified. Not later, when you are no longer
struggling. Don't wait until you're no longer broken.

Stop thinking about grace and put grace into action. Start respond-
ing to God's love—instead of other's expectations of what is beautiful
or good enough.

Open your heart and step out *now.* Choose grace and be the
bold, beloved you.

✑ *God's Whispers to You*

Beloved,
You were made to bring beautiful things into the world.
Yes. You are your Father's daughter. You are just like me.

When feelings of guilt and shame threaten to silence you,
whisper my name. Feel my strong arms holding you close.
I'll reassure you again and again. Your heart is my throne.

My grace, like love's eternal flame, can never be extinguished
in you. I am faithful. Willing to help you and give you grace in
your time of need.

Your art, your voice matters. You matter.
Let my grace in, not guilt.

You matter to God. Don't wait until the critical voices die
down. Do your art. Be you. Now. As is.

☞ A Prayer for Today:
Let Grace In Instead of Guilt

"Let us then approach God's throne of grace with
confidence, so that we may receive mercy and find
grace to help us in our time of need."   HEBREWS 4:16

Dear Jesus,
Give me courage to let grace in, instead of guilt.

Thank you for the seeds of inspiration you've planted in my heart.
For your whispers of love that never cease.
Even in my greatest moments of weakness.

Moment after moment, I need your grace.
Every hour. Help me in my time of need.
Thank you. Amen.

Give Yourself Permission: Do your art in small ways. Be bold. Stop living to quiet your critics. Choose grace. Let go of shame. Do one thing you enjoy today. Be curious. Begin again.

REFLECT ON YOUR STORY

1. *What would you change or start, if you allowed yourself to be more human, imperfect but loved, and gave yourself more grace?*

2. *Which of the Four Whispers of Grace speaks to you today?*

3. *What One Word speaks to you today?*

PRAY & REST

A SIMPLE PRACTICE: PRAY FOR GRACE NOW

You don't have to feel guilty for asking for grace (again) to meet today's demands. You can have *fresh grace*, every moment you need it. Sometimes, we say, "I don't want to bother God. I'll just suck it up for now and pray later when I feel better." Theologian Ray Stedman shares, "There is a tendency for Christians to think of heaven as 'out there'...to address an appeal somewhere in space. The throne of grace is not a remote space; it is right in the heart in whom Jesus dwells—in us."

Today's One Word Prayer is *GRACE*. Pray *now* for God's fresh grace. Don't wait. His grace is a *river*, flowing abundantly to replenish you continuously. It never runs out. It brings God joy to free your heart with grace!

Dear Jesus, I feel guilty for . . .

But I feel inspired to_____, and I ask for fresh grace right now to . . .

TODAY'S BELOVED CHALLENGE

What's Your Craft?
Make Something with Your Hands
Find your flow and free your heart.

Let grace in, not guilt. Be inspired by God's love for you today.

SOUL CARE TRAIL NOTES

Be Present by Making Something

Asking for God's grace invites us to be present. One thing that helps us to be present and experience rest is by making things with our hands.

Our nervous system can handle processing only a certain amount of information before we're overwhelmed, triggering a "flight or flight" response of stress and anxiety. The repetitive motions of creating with our hands—whether drawing, playing music, cooking, music, photography, or gardening—returns calm to the nervous system. We enter a state of "flow," similar to meditation, easing stress, increasing happiness, and activating dopamine, a natural mood enhancer. One study of 3,500 people with depression found that 81 percent of them reported feeling happy after knitting!

PART THREE

Dreaming as the Beloved

❧ ❧ ❧

Rejuvenate Your Passion for Life

As you make choices that reflect your self-worth,
God's love will awaken your dreams again.

Jesus whispers,
Don't despise small beginnings.
You are big in my eyes.

The following devotionals inspire you
to rejuvenate your passion for life—
and rediscover your God-Breathed dreams.

God will recover whatever has been lost
and you will find your passion again.

"Do not despise small beginnings,
for the Lord rejoices to see the work begin."

ZECHARIAH 4:10

Gather

God-Breathed Dreams

The dream you dare whisper, I hear.

Just like Ruth never expected
she would find a Boaz
while gathering leftovers
in the fields for Naomi,
you are not forgotten.

The dream you dare to whisper in private—God hears.

*"I have loved you with an everlasting love;
I have drawn you with unfailing kindness."*

JEREMIAH 31:3

*"We must never stop dreaming. Dreams provide nour-
ishment for the soul, just as a meal does for the body."*

PAULO COELHO

It happens at night when it's quiet. When the moon climbs up
over the mountains and peeks through my window, the part of
me who dreams emerges.

When I was single, I asked, *Is there someone to hold me forever?
To say he'll love me—who will warm my body and my soul—and stay
the way God meant it to be?* As a wife now, other dreams I once
brushed aside as a little girl, like seashells returning to shore,
are washing back to me.

Is this true for you, too? Do you find whenever it's quiet—
when you watch the leaves fall like blossoms in autumn or
when the morning light warms the room—your heart whispers dreams overlooked in the busyness of life?

Is it a baby you long for, a marriage, friendship or community, a family mended, or home? Is your dream a passion or
idea you want to make real, a business, ministry, or adventure
to explore? Maybe your dream is healing for your body or your
heart—the way you feel about yourself?

God-Breathed Dreams

Like seeds scattered in the wind, dreams can lie dormant, lost
or broken. Life may seem easier without our dreams. But we
weren't made to simply do life as maintenance. *There are God-
Breathed Dreams planted in each of us that are still alive, even if we've
left them behind.*

When God takes us on the journey to revitalize our soul,

God renews His dreams for you as His Beloved. Will you whisper your dreams to God again? Return to a tender place in your heart where dreams lay bare.

Just like Ruth never expected she would find a Boaz while gathering leftovers in the fields for Naomi, you are not forgotten. The dream you dare to whisper in private—God hears. You are not overlooked.

Like Ruth, you are focusing on the gathering—the work that's right in front of you. You get up and lie down, faithful to work hard and encourage those around you. Yet, there is a soulful, deeper part of you God sees. The part of you who dreams.

Is there really a place for your dreams in this world? Changes will be needed. Where will this journey take you?

We may be afraid to leave what we know. But there comes a time we must gather our courage to dream again—even if it seems all we have are leftovers. Because, you see, God sees leftovers differently. *God sees you.*

Gather

Gather. This was one word a woman once whispered to herself. Ruth didn't fit in—she was young, widowed, and poor—in a foreign country. She didn't have any real means or outward significance. She looked at all her options and she decided she needed to go into the fields. All she could do was gather. Leftovers.

Some might have looked at Ruth's life and shook their heads, sighing at the story written in her circumstances. But the woman God saw and knew was very different.

So God left us an intimate story about leftovers. About leaving. About *gathering behind others.* So that we would come to understand that we aren't so lost in His world.

▰▰▰ READ GOD'S STORY ▰▰▰

Come. Jesus invites us to step into Ruth's story. See her steadying her courage to gather leftovers. To put herself at risk of hurt or shame.

So Ruth went and entered a field
and gathered the grain left behind the reapers.

Now it happened that she ended up
in the part of the field that belonged to Boaz.

Just then, Boaz was coming from Bethlehem...
Boaz asked the young man in charge of his reapers,
"Who is this young woman?"

The man answered...
"She came here and has been on her feet
from daybreak until now.
She just sat down this minute in the shelter."

At mealtime Boaz said to her,
"Come here, that you may eat of the bread
and dip your piece of bread in the vinegar."
So she sat beside the reapers;
and he served her roasted grain,
and she ate and was satisfied.

RUTH 2:2–17

Happenstance

Do you see Ruth gleaning among a field she "happened to end up in"?
This phrase translated in the original language reads "and her

chance, chanced." In Hebrew text, repetition is used to create irony, to indicate the opposite meaning.

There was simply no chance, if any, Ruth could possibly end up in that particular field, just as Boaz was there, at the minute *she happened to be resting*. God orchestrated this opportunity.

God knew the dreams in her heart. But Ruth had to take the risk. *Ruth had to leave, go, gather and rest.* Even as Ruth gathered the leftovers—behind all the other reapers—God loved Ruth. And God loves *you*.

✍ *God's Whispers to You*

Beloved,
I see you. From sunup to sundown you are gathering.
Don't be afraid. I love you.

I have a plan. Chance upon chance.
I will orchestrate the opportunities for my dreams for you.

I am in control of your destiny.
Let me be your shelter. Let me be your shade.

✍ *A Prayer for Today:*
When You Long to Dream Again

"I have loved you with an everlasting love;
I have drawn you with unfailing kindness."

JEREMIAH 31:3

Dear Jesus,
Chance upon chance, I'm trusting you.

Give me courage to gather today
what you've put in my path.

I will go where you lead me,
to find new dreams as your Beloved.

Give me courage to leave
relationships, places or expectations I once felt resigned to.

Gather with me, Jesus.
Be my shelter. Be my shade.

Give Yourself Permission: Whisper your God-Breathed Dreams again. Take one step to go, gather and explore a dream. No matter how small. Leave what's familiar behind.

REFLECT ON YOUR STORY

1. *What are your God-Breathed Dreams?*

2. *Where are you in this story? How is God prompting you to go, gather, leave, move out, or rest—to experience kindness?*

3. *What One Word speaks to you today?*

PRAY & REST

A SIMPLE PRACTICE: STILLNESS PRAYER

"Be still and know that I am God." In *Invitation to Solitude and Silence*, Ruth Haley Barton writes, "Psalm 46:10 tells us there is a kind of knowing that comes in silence and not in words—but first we must be still. The Hebrew word translated 'Be still' literally means 'Let go of your grip.'"

Today, practice stillness. Put aside your work and worries for now. Relax in God's presence. Begin praying by whispering, "Be still." Using today's One Word Prayer, *GATHER*, look back on your dreams, past or present. Gather any words of encouragement God is saying to you. Ask the Holy Spirit to guide you.

Write the encouragement you've gleaned in stillness here . . .

— 🥐 🥐 🥐 —

TODAY'S BELOVED CHALLENGE

Think Happy Memories

Find an old photo that makes you smile.
Share it or simply savor that memory.

On days you hardly have time to breathe, recall something that made you happy. Gather the moments God whispered, *I love you.*

SOUL CARE TRAIL NOTES

Old Photos Self-Soothe and Improve Mood

The act of gleaning is a wonderful reminder to look for grains of encouragement when they're hard to find. When you're feeling down, recall something that made you happy. Simply recalling that memory produces the happy hormone serotonin, increasing a sense of well-being.

Look through old photos of your kids, sister, friend, or husband, or your last vacation. UK's Open University examined how much people's moods rose after eating a chocolate snack, watching TV, or looking at personal photos. They found that chocolate left most people's moods unchanged and TV gave a slight lift, but viewing personal photos gave people the biggest boost.

ᗩ ᗩ ᗩ

Guide

God-Guided Dreams

This is the way. Walk in it. My love will guide you.

Sometimes, we wait for a plan to emerge.
But love doesn't work that way.

Jesus whispers instead:
Take my hand.
I will be your bread for this journey.
My love will guide you.

*"Whether you turn to the right or to the left, your ears
will hear a voice behind you, saying, 'This is the way;
Walk in it.'"*   ISAIAH 30:21

"I was not sure where I was going, and I could not see...
But you saw further...led me across the waters to a
place I had never dreamed of, and which you were even
then preparing for me to be my rescue and my shelter
and my home."

THOMAS MERTON

My friend Carol lives on a ranch in Montana.

Blue skies stretch out like a canopy, as horses roam across mountains that unfold like fresh dough resting before it rises. This land is wild. And the rivers that run through it in spring rush down fast and furious.

Carol tells me this as I call her from California, where the drought has worn long and deep. I'm not just talking about creek beds running dry. It's the landscape of my heart that I'm confiding to my friend.

I tell her that the plans I felt so sure God designed for me unexpectedly fell through. I'm stuck at a fork in the road. It's not clear which way I should go.

"Why would God lead me so clearly to this point in my journey—only to have plans unravel so badly?" I ask her. "I don't know what God wants me to do. I'm so confused."

Are you searching for God's voice—for His direction? Have your plans changed course unexpectedly? Are you thirsting for a word of guidance from Him today?

Let me tell you what Carol told me that day.

Moving the Water

Carol's neighbor lives four miles away. One night, he knocked on her door. He said water would be arriving in twenty-four hours to water her land.

He told her *he would move the water tonight.* It's an unusual phrase. It turns out that Carol's neighbor, who lives upstream from her, is the gatekeeper for the reservoir holding all the water that supplies what farmers and ranchers need downstream. The gatekeeper watches the waters swell and he reads the weather in the clouds.

"Moving the water" meant he would open a series of gates and *release the water to run where it was most needed to replenish the land.* If the land wasn't getting enough water, he would rearrange the gates to redistribute its flow.

"Changes in your life," Carol told me, "are how God opens gates in our hearts—to release the things that need to be let go in order to bring new life to areas we can't see but God sees."

God changes the direction in our lives, not to harm us but to bring new life.

> *"For I know the plans I have for you…not to harm you,*
> *plans to give you hope and a future."*   JEREMIAH 29:11

God-Guided Dreams

A change in direction feels scary in the moment, but it leads us to our *God-Guided Dreams.* God sees the way ahead. But we need to trust Him and make room for Him first. *God can only speak to us best when we allow Him room to guide us ahead.*

Sometimes to hear God's voice, we need to first open the gates in our hearts that we've kept closed. We need to *surrender* our plan and our will. We often want to know God's direction first before surrendering. But God sees the needs in our lives. This is how a heart runs wild and free again, friend: by letting go.

Like the intimate moment when a woman lets a man in close to love her, let us soften our hearts. Let us surrender to our God-Guided Dreams. Let us take the first step to let go of the plans that hold on to us. As we do, we will hear God's voice of love speak to us again, sweet like the spring's first raindrops again.

> *"I am the good shepherd…*
> *The gatekeeper opens the gate for him and the sheep*
> *listen for his voice…*
> *He goes before them and they follow him."*
>
> JOHN 10:3, 4, 11

READ GOD'S STORY

Slow down. Savor stillness now. Like a cloud moving across the sky, pause along your journey. Let God's words move gently across where you stand. Just like Moses felt the brush of God pass by him as he hid in the cleft of a rock—*feel God's nearness.* Listen to Him speak to you from Isaiah 30:19–23:

> *"You will weep no longer.*
> *He will surely be gracious to you at the sound of your cry;*
> *when He hears it, He will answer you…*
>
> *He, your Teacher, will no longer hide Himself,*
> *but your eyes will behold your Teacher.*
>
> *Your ears will hear a word behind you,*
> *'This is the way, walk in it,'*
> *whenever you turn to the right or to the left.*
>
> *Then He will give you rain for the seed which you will sow*
> *in the ground, and bread from the yield of the ground, and*
> *it will be rich and plenteous."*   ISAIAH 30:19–23

✍ *God's Whispers to You*

Beloved,
When you're unsure and afraid, I will make a way to you.
I won't give up on you. I won't leave you to wander.

And if you falter, I'll keep whispering it, close to your ear:
This is the way—Beloved. Walk in it.

No matter how small or insignificant each step feels,
Take my hand.
I will be your bread for this journey.
I will give you rain for the seed of dreams in you.
My love will guide you.

✍ *A Prayer for Today:*
When You Don't Know Which Way to Turn

"Whether you turn to the right or to the left,
your ears will hear a voice behind you, saying,
'This is the way; Walk in it.'"   ISAIAH 30:21

Dear Jesus,
Guide me, Lord.
I surrender my plans to hold on to you.
Don't hide. I need to see you in this.
Don't be silent. I need to hear you.

Give me courage to trust you
and faith to act on your whispers.
Thank you for being faithful.

Giving me your word. Right when I need it.
Amen.

Give Yourself Permission: When your dreams stall, choose the path that guides you to experience God's love and peace best. Surrender. Rest, wait and listen. Trust that God's next-step whisper comes after your step of faith.

REFLECT ON YOUR STORY

1. *What areas are you seeking God's guidance?*

2. *What One Word speaks to you in today's Scriptures?*

PRAY & REST

A SIMPLE PRACTICE: PRAYING THE SCRIPTURES

Today, we practice a contemplative prayer presented by Madame Guyon in her classic book *Experiencing the Depths of Jesus Christ*. "Praying the Scripture involves both reading and prayer. Come quietly before him. Read a small portion *very slowly*. Do not move from one passage to another, until you sense the very heart of what you have read. Take [what] has touched you and turn it into prayer. Praying the Scripture is not judged by how much you read, *but the way you read it*. Little by little, you will experience a very rich prayer that flowers from your inward being."

How does God's voice sound reading today's passage (Isaiah 30:19–23)—gentle or soft? Which words draw you in? How do they make you feel? Let His Holy Spirit speak. Meditate on today's One Word Prayer, *GUIDE. Write your prayer now . . .*

TODAY'S BELOVED CHALLENGE

Savor Something Delicious

Sit and eat slowly. Enjoy your food.
Don't multitask. Be present. Breathe.

Live today fully. God's love will guide you.

Eat More Slowly and Experience Rest

SOUL CARE
TRAIL
NOTES

When we *savor* God's word slowly, we enjoy being with Him. It's like eating slower, to taste the flavors and breathe, rather than gobbling food down.

Our hectic, fast-paced life leads to stressful, unhealthy living, as we rush through our day, unhappy and mindlessly running through our tasks, eating on the run. By choosing the simple act of eating slower, you take time to live, enjoy life, relate to others, and experience more rest. Studies show benefits of the Slow Food movement include losing weight (it takes twenty minutes for your brain to register you're full), good digestion (better health) and less stress. Eating slowly practices mindfulness and frees you to be in the moment rather than worry about what's next.

Carry

God-Created Dreams

My Presence will go with you. I will carry you.

We may be uncertain about our next steps,
but we can be certain of God's hand in ours.
And He's not letting go.

God whispers,
My Presence will go with you. I will give you rest.
I know your name. I will carry you.

"Even to your old age, I will be the same. I have made
you and I will carry you. I will sustain you and I will
rescue you." ISAIAH 46:4

"My Presence will go with you and I will give you rest."

EXODUS 33:14, 17

"I will go where there is no path, and I will leave a trail."

I never used to be afraid. I was all faith. Or so I thought.

I had enough faith for everyone around me, and seconds to go around too. *Everything would always work out fine because I was with Jesus. And Jesus was with me.*

I loved people, prayed, studied my Bible, and recycled regularly. But as time passed and the number of things that went wrong started adding up, I unconsciously started keeping a tally. I never would've admitted I was keeping such a list. Not even to myself, much less to God. But I did.

Deep in my heart, I had a running list of questions about where God was leading me. And why it was taking so long. *I've carried dreams deferred*—dreams about what was my purpose or calling.

I trusted God, but it seemed every year my dreams moved farther away from me. I began to despair.

God-Created Dreams

Of course, I knew that God is all good, all knowing, and powerful. So I didn't allow myself to doubt God's plans for me. Or so I thought.

I masked my insecurities with God by doubting myself. What I feared most was being forgotten. I was afraid to live an insignificant life.

Do you have dreams deferred, hidden in your heart? God sees the heartbeat in each dream grown faint but still beating. God wants you to know He understands the sense of despair you feel when dreams fade.

"Hope deferred makes the heart sick,
but a longing fulfilled is a tree of life."   PROVERBS 13:12

Be encouraged. God values faith in ways we least expect. Our life is hidden in Christ. Where we see nothingness, God is birthing *God-Created Dreams* in us.

READ GOD'S STORY

During a weekend away spent in spiritual whitespace—time alone to feed my soul—I decided to write down a list of all my disappointments with God. After writing pages and pages, God lovingly brought four pictures to mind.

Step into these four pictures of *God-Created Dreams*. Find yourself in one.

1. *In the beginning, there was nothing.*

   Now the earth was formless and empty, darkness was over the surface of the deep, and the Spirit of God was moving over the waters. And God said, "Let there be light," and there was light.

   GENESIS 1:2–3

   It was in nothing the Holy Spirit hovered, where God created something.

2. *I'm not qualified. I can't see how this will work*, Moses confessed.

   "My presence will go with you and I will give you rest…
   I know your name."   EXODUS 33:14, 17

   When nothing ahead was certain, God's presence led the way.

3. *I'm too broken. It's too late*, a weary Israel despaired.

> *"Even to your old age, I will be the same. I have made you and I will carry you. I will sustain you and I will rescue you."*
>
> ISAIAH 46:4

When no rescue can be found, God carries the one He loves.

Nothingness. *That's me!* A bolt of lightning struck my heart and resuscitated my story.

God continues His beautiful, creative work in you today. In your heart—where deferred dreams remain—contains the very space God is birthing new dreams again. A God-Created Dream in you.

In the everyday, God's presence is at work in us. In the everyday, Jesus leads us to dreams we can't yet see. I realized the best life—the most significant life we can live—is the one we grow in faith today.

✐ *God's Whispers to You*

Beloved,
Next time you feel overwhelmed by areas in your life that
  appear dark and formless—remember I am faithful—
to create something beautiful in you,
to carry you to safety,
to make a way you cannot see,
to put you back together again,
to return laughter where you taste sorrow,
to give you courage to start over (again and again),
and use every loss and every triumph for my love for you.

My Presence is with you. I will give you rest.
I know your name. I will carry you.

✍ *A Prayer for Today:*
When You Need God to Carry You

"Even to your old age, I will be the same.
I have made you and I will carry you.
I will sustain you and I will rescue you."   ISAIAH 46:4

"My presence will go with you and I will give you rest."
                                    EXODUS 33:14, 17

Dear Jesus,
I'm weary by my dreams, deferred so long.

Take my empty spaces.
Fill the void with your Holy Spirit.
Have your way in me. A God-Created Dream.
Help me to believe.

I don't know what to do, but you do.
Show me, and I will follow.
Go with me. I want the better dream.
You, Jesus, your loving presence is all I need.

Carry me, when I can't go further.
Thank you for loving me.
Amen.

Next time you think nothing is happening in your life—
or you find yourself asking, "How can this be?"—remember
things aren't as they appear.

Jesus sees you. And he will never forget why he put you
here.

Give Yourself Permission: Rather than looking for God's will in the future, find out what God has for you in today's circumstances. Let God change your story. Start over. Begin imperfectly, right where you are, perfectly loved.

REFLECT ON YOUR STORY

1. *What new dream is being created in you?*

2. *How is God encouraging you in your faith?*

3. *What One Word speaks to you today?*

PRAY & REST

A SIMPLE PRACTICE: PRAY GOD'S PROMISES

Today, let's pray God's promises to revive His dreams for us. Charles Spurgeon, England's well-known preacher, writes, "Instead of trying to revive yourself, offer prayers. 'O Lord, revive thy work.' You do not need new ways or new people. You need life in what you have. You need to light a fire." Spurgeon used God's promise in Habakkuk 3:2 to light up and carry his prayer.

What promise in Scripture carries you? Turn it into your prayer. Use the examples below or write your own. Meditate on today's One Word Prayer, *CARRY:*

"earth was formless, the Spirit moved" (Genesis 1:2)	*Bring order into my chaos.*
"God said let there be light" (Genesis 1:3)	*Bring light into my darkness.*
"Nothing is impossible" (Luke 1:37)	*Let it be with me as you say.*
"I will carry you" (Isaiah 46:4)	*Carry me.*
Pray God's promise for you here . . .	

TODAY'S BELOVED CHALLENGE

Hug Someone

God created us to need touch.
Hugging relaxes our body and revitalizes the soul.

Be encouraged. God holds you close. He will carry you today.

SOUL CARE TRAIL NOTES

Hugging Relaxes and Improves Your Mood

God created us to need touch, even as adults. He even promises to carry us into old age. When you're feeling down, hug someone. When we hug, the pressure stimulates receptors under our skin, releasing oxytocin—relaxing the body (this hormone draws mothers to nurture their babies), reducing the stress hormone cortisol, blood pressure, and heart rate. Sheldon Cohen, professor of psychology at Carnegie Mellon University, says hugging "is a marker of intimacy and helps generate the feeling that others are there to help in the face of adversity."

DAY 18

❧ ❧ ❧

Small

A Greater Dream

Don't despise small beginnings. You are big in my eyes.

Nothing too big is impossible for God.
More importantly,
nothing is too small is impossible for God, either.

Your dreams are safe with Jesus—
Don't despise small beginnings.
You are big in my eyes.
I will never be parted from you.
You are everything beautiful to me.

"Do not despise these small beginnings,
for the Lord rejoices to see the work begin."

ZECHARIAH 4:10

"Faithfulness in small things is how God grows something of lasting importance." LAMBERT DOLPHIN

When we're tempted to look back and think our best days are behind us, God knows better.

Every once in a while, I like to clean out my closets and drawers. I'll suddenly be struck with the urge to purge. *This weekend, I'm staying home and getting organized. I'm getting rid of stuff!*

What inevitably happens is I get derailed, stumbling on photos, trinkets, or loose papers. I'll end up sitting there, surrounded by clutter, reminiscing. *I sure looked young back in college. Not a care. Wrinkle-free... There I am, fired up to change the world for Christ... Oh, there's my Jeep. Untethered by responsibilities, we drove wherever we wanted to go.*

Most of all, I'd longingly look into my innocent smile. Life was wide open. But now, my hands hold more baggage, my heart bears scars, and my soul is no longer a stranger to fears and insecurities. Sometimes I can fall into the trap of thinking that I'm simply an older, not-so-shiny version of Bonnie.

On a bad day, we can feel like our best is already behind us. We can stare into our daily schedule, and it feels quite ordinary. Life doesn't always work out the way we expected.

Even though you can love your life, thankful for all God's blessings, you may feel the way I sometimes do. *Small.* Ordinary.

It's too late, we tell ourselves. We feel our small efforts to begin something new can't match the vision of what we want.

God loves us too much to let us wane in atrophy and discouragement. God sees something totally different that captures His heart: beautiful you.

The Dream, the Vision

God understands how things might appear small to us compared to others in our private moments. About our bodies, our relationships, our plans, and our futures—and how we give up on our dreams.

God steps in quietly to lead us back to a time when His people gave up on their dreams, too. *He brings our attention to the story of the building of the second temple.*

The first temple King Solomon built was decked out in gold, an amazing architectural achievement—bringing glory to Jerusalem, with nations streaming afar to visit. But when the Israelites returned to rebuild the temple—while under captivity—it was a very faded version of its famed original.

The city was actually lying in ruins. The walls would not even be rebuilt for years. Older men who had seen the splendor of Solomon's Temple thought this second temple looked pretty sorry and insignificant (Ezra 3:10–13).

They cried and wailed in sadness and disappointment. They ripped their clothes as a sign of mourning when someone dies. *The dream of who they once were and their vision of what could have been died.*

What was God's response?

READ GOD'S STORY

Hear God whisper to you now.

> "Do not despise these small beginnings,
> for the Lord rejoices to see the work begin.
> …[My] hands will also complete it.

But now, take courage. For I am with you.
My Spirit remains among you; do not fear!

I will fill this temple with glory.
The glory of this latter temple shall be greater than the
former. and in this place I will give peace."

ZECHARIAH 4:9–10, HAGGAI 2:4–9

Do not despise small beginnings. God encourages us. God uses the small and creates the best with us. Whatever is ahead of you will be *greater* than anything ever before, even if it doesn't look that way on the outside.

Like me, the people got it wrong. They valued the temple based on *what it looked like*, rather than on *the God who was dwelling in it.*

God's Greater Dream for You

What makes you and your dreams beautiful isn't how things appear. What makes you beautiful is who lives in you. *You are the beautiful, glorious temple of the living God* (see 1 Corinthians 6:19). You are His home.

This is God's Greater Dream for you: His presence. Beauty within. Not what appears on the outside. God's Greater Dream for you is more powerful than any circumstance you can find yourself in: His very Spirit dwells in you.

What makes you beautiful is God's very hand moving within you in *the small moments*—with peace, joy, and beauty. God's love is a seed blossoming—through the ideas and dreams He inspires in you—an inner beauty glowing that far exceeds anything we've lost in the past.

Be assured. God is faithful. He will not abandon the work

of hands. God says, "I will complete this work in you." You belong to Him.

"Being confident of this,
that he who began a good work in you will complete it."

PHILIPPIANS 1:6

✐ *God's Whispers to You*

Beloved,
When you feel like your best dreams have faded,
think of me. The best days are ahead of you.
My dreams in you can never be destroyed.

My dream for you will blossom and grow.
Because that Greater Dream is me—coming alive in you.

Do not despise small beginnings.
You are big in my eyes.
I'll never be parted from you.
You are everything beautiful to me. Today.

Our best days are ahead of us because the great God we follow is ahead of us. Nothing too big is impossible for God. More important—*nothing is too small is impossible for God, either.*

The beauty of faith isn't measured by how far you've walked or what you've accomplished. It's found in the Person walking with you. Your dreams are safe with Jesus. He will never be parted from you.

✑ *A Prayer for Today*: *When You Feel Small*

"Do not despise these small beginnings,
for the Lord rejoices to see the work begin."

ZECHARIAH 4:10

Dear Jesus,
Give me courage to treasure small beginnings
in myself and others in my life,
To look beyond how things appear.
To choose the beauty of small moments,
because you are intimately at work creating lovely things within.

Rather than striving and stressing,
comparing myself to what was or ought to be,
help me rest in your love for me today.

Free my heart to pursue a Greater Dream with you,
to come alive in your very presence—
and fully enjoy whatever you invite me into today.

Thank you.
Amen.

Give Yourself Permission: Stop comparing yourself to who you were in the past, who you wish you could be in the future, or anyone else today. Value who you are right now. Take a small step to enjoy what makes you feel most alive. Begin again.

REFLECT ON YOUR STORY

1. *How do you feel about yourself today? What is God's view?*

2. *What is a small beginning—a Greater Dream—that God is inviting you to experience with Him?*

3. *What One Word speaks to you today?*

PRAY & REST

A SIMPLE PRACTICE: SAY YES TO SMALL MOMENTS

Today's prayer practice is inspired by John Ortberg, author of *Soul Keeping*: "*The best place to start doing life with God is in small moments.* So I take a little time during prayer to just listen... and practice saying yes."

As you enter into prayer now, breathe in slowly. As you breathe out—let go of the big responsibilities, goals or tasks. Put them aside for the moment. Reflect on today's One Word Prayer, *SMALL*. What small moment is God inviting you to enjoy alone with Him or with others today? What small beginning is God calling you to value and see? Listen. Then, say *yes*.

Jesus, thank you for inviting me to small moments. I will say yes to . . .

───── 🍃 🍃 🍃 ─────

TODAY'S BELOVED CHALLENGE

Notice the Small Things
Engage Your Five Senses:
sight, smell, sound, taste, and touch.

Don't despise small beginnings. You are big in God's eyes. He loves you.

SOUL CARE TRAIL NOTES

Engage Your Five Senses to Relax

Small moments help us relieve stress, offering a powerful relaxation technique: engaging our senses. Studies show that engaging the five senses improves our mood and brings calm—as everyday demands disconnect our minds from our bodies (resulting in stress and anxiety).

Seeing beautiful images or colors in nature like blue, green, and earth tones soothes and energizes. Sounds in nature or music offer effective mood therapy. Calming scents like jasmine lowers heart rates, savoring tastes like tea or chocolate triggers happiness, and the touch from a hug, a shower, or a hands-on hobby brings comfort.

DAY 19

≈ ≈ ≈

Plant

New Dreams

I will restore you. You can dream again.

In every woman God made
lies the quiet bloom of a little girl.
And behind every dream lost
lies *new dreams* waiting to be found.

God plants dreams in you to whisper,
You are my beloved.
I will restore you.
You can dream again.

*"The threshing floors will be filled with grain
and the vats will overflow with new wine and oil.
I will restore to you the years that the swarming locust
has eaten."*   JOEL 2:24–25

152

"Don't dig up in doubt what you planted in faith."

ELISABETH ELLIOT

When you were little, life was a blank canvas. You could do or be anything. Now that you've grown up, maybe you're wondering if new dreams can ever grow again.

My friend John told me a story that encouraged me so much I'd like to share it with you. John is a psychologist. He didn't know a thing about Sumo oranges, a sweet, seedless tangerine hybrid that took thirty years to develop in Japan. But his father was a farmer who—after decades of growing olive trees and navel oranges in California—decided to pull up all the trees in one orchard he purchased and invest in planting the new Asian citrus fruit.

Four months later, John's father died. John was left staring into fields he never farmed before. The ground was bare.

You couldn't tell anything new had been planted. But John didn't sell the land. *He kept investing in his father's dream.* Paid the bills to water the seeds and hired a grower to work the ground.

The first year, the seeds grew into saplings. The second year, the branches began to bud and blossom. First flowers. *But still there was no fruit.*

What John told me next sparked new dreams God once planted in my heart years ago, but I'd felt too discouraged to nurture again.

What's amazing is this: *Fruit does not come until after the blossoms bloom and fall to the ground.* No dreams are wasted in God's hand. He puts your tears in a bottle to water something beautiful and new in you.

"You keep track of all my sorrows.
You have collected all my tears in your bottle."

PSALM 56:8

Not only that, in the third year, when the first fruits finally arrive, they cannot be eaten. They are too green and too little. They need to be let go. *The first fruits have to fall to the ground.* The farmers thin the oranges so they can grow big later.

It's the same with our dreams. Where we suffer failure, God assures us: *Don't give up. This isn't your end.*

"Those who go out weeping, carrying seed to sow,
will return with songs of joy, carrying sheaves with them."

PSALM 126:6

Finally, in the fourth year, the citrus fruit trees ripen to succulent sweetness. Seeds that once lay dormant wake up to bear branches bursting full of delicious new fruit in fields once empty. They can be enjoyed and eaten!

New Dreams

How about you? Having gone through barren winters, false-start springtimes, or green-fruit summers, are there new dreams that God wants you to plant and nurture—even though it seems so completely opposite to what you've ever done?

Just like my friend John, who took care of fields that looked barren but were full of new seeds his father planted, keep investing in the new dreams that your Heavenly Father planted in you. Don't give up. Sometimes, when you least expect it—after you've already resigned yourself to stop dreaming—God stirs your heart. *Awaken to the life of faith in you. New dreams will start to grow.*

Where do we start? Are we too late? But how? And when—now?

Questions and doubts are a part of faith coming alive, pointing you to something new. Just don't push that moment of inspiration and longing away because of them. Draw nearer to Jesus, confiding in all that's hidden in your heart.

READ GOD'S STORY

Come. As you are. *See.* What Jesus longs to show you. *Listen.* To Jesus share about how things grow in his kingdom, in your soul, where he lives today:

> *"This is what God's kingdom is like.*
> *It's as though someone scatters seed on the ground,*
> *then sleeps and wakes, night and day.*
>
> > *The seed sprouts and grows,*
> > *but the farmer doesn't know how.*
>
> *The earth produces crops all by itself,*
> *first the stalk, then the head,*
> *then the full head of grain.*
>
> > *Whenever the crop is ready,*
> > *the farmer goes out to cut the grain*
> > *because it's harvest time."*
> > MARK 4:26–29

Are you carrying a dream that you've tried to bury and forget? Maybe like seeds hidden in the soil, God is nourishing you with comfort and kindness, where critical voices abandoned you to numb your heart.

Have you grown weary in the waiting? Maybe you've come close, blossoms in bloom. Yet fruit has eluded you.

Be encouraged. *Jesus invites you to lay down your burden today and dream again.* Jesus calls you to return to the field where his kingdom reigns: your heart. He loves you. *You were made to bear fruit.*

✑ God's Whispers to You

Beloved,
I will restore the years the locusts have eaten.
Don't give up. The dreams you once tried to forget,
I haven't forgotten. I haven't forgotten you.

Don't be afraid. You are good soil.
I've walked the broken journey
so you don't have to toil in fear to do more,
be more, or abandon yourself to being invisible.

It's time to water. Plant new seeds.
There is a season for everything.
Winter, spring, summer, or fall, I love every part of you.
You are my Beloved. You can dream again.

It may seem easier to bury your heart underneath all the busyness. But in the heart of every woman lies the quiet bloom of a little girl. Behind every dream lost lies new dreams waiting to be found.

✑ A Prayer for Today: For Courage to Plant New Dreams

"The threshing floors will be filled with grain
and the vats will overflow with new wine and oil.
I will restore to you the years that the swarming locust
has eaten."   JOEL 2:24–25

Dear Jesus,
Give me the courage to remember what it's like to dream again.
Help me to find my voice when I'm tempted to hide.

I've tried so hard to make things grow on my own
because I've been afraid to let go of what has been.
Help me to open my heart again. To plant new seeds.
Breathe life into my heart so I can believe:
you can make beautiful things in me again.

Help me be that little girl who comes alive with your joy.
I surrender to the new journey you have for me.
Remake my dreams. Love me deeper today.
Amen.

Love will carry that seed of God's dreams for you to blossom, just as He first imagined you lit up by the quiet whispers He spoke into your heart—*I love you.*

Give Yourself Permission: Join God to plant a new dream: till the soil, plant new seeds, water and wait, bloom first blossoms, collect first fruits, or harvest. Grieve the dreams that have been lost or destroyed.

REFLECT ON YOUR STORY

1. *How is God inviting you to plant a new dream or nurture one in your heart?*

2. *What One Word in today's Scripture speaks to you?*

PRAY & REST

A SIMPLE PRACTICE: MEDITATIVE PRAYER—USE YOUR IMAGINATION

Richard Foster calls *Meditative Prayer* seeking to *experience* Scripture: "Meditation on scripture centers on...*personalizing* the passage...we come to God with mind and heart. The simplest way to meditate is through imagination. We enter the story and make it our own...to see, hear, touch the biblical narrative."

For today's Meditative Prayer, imagine yourself with Jesus in today's passage of Mark 4:26–29. Jesus left the crowds and was alone with his disciples enjoying a private conversation. How do you feel when he tells you the story? What questions arise? Reflect on today's One Word Prayer, *PLANT.*

Jesus, when I imagine myself here with you, saying these words to me, I feel...

—— 𝒟 𝒟 𝒟 ——

TODAY'S BELOVED CHALLENGE

Take a Fruit Break
Enjoy your favorite fruit.
Savor the sweetness. Make your body happy.

Take a break. Eat something sweet God designed to naturally energize and refresh you, and keep you healthy.

SOUL CARE TRAIL NOTES

Eating Fruit Helps Combat Stress

Our One Word Prayer is an easy way to return to God and get refreshed with His peace when we're stressed. Another way to get refreshed is by taking a fruit break. Fruit not only strengthens our immune system, helping fight colds, but vitamin C also help us bounce back from stressful situations faster.

German researchers tested this by asking people to give a speech, then do hard math problems. Those given vitamin C had lower blood pressures and lower levels of the stress hormone cortisol. Citrus is high in Vitamin C. Blueberries—as well as strawberries, raspberries, and black berries—also are rich in vitamin C and have the highest levels of antioxidants. Two cups meets the daily average need.

≈ ≈ ≈

Shelter

Nurturing Dreams

Let me be your shelter. You belong with me.

Every dream nurtured
can unlock everything beautiful
in your heart with Jesus.

Jesus whispers—
I will be your shelter. Rest and refresh.
Let me be your shade. Today.

"You are my shelter and my shield
I put my hope in your word."   PSALM 119:114

"I have spread my dreams under your feet;
Tread softly because you tread on my dreams."

No matter what was happening, he was always there to greet me. He wasn't a man but a willow tree.

My willow tree was planted next to a playground in the neighborhood park, surrounded by cracked cement. I'd run a few laps in the tanbark, pushing the squeaky metal merry-go-round. Then, I'd hop on, spin myself dizzy, my hair like a pinwheel twirling in the wind.

During sweltering summers, I'd rest under the willow, when the steel slides were too hot to touch. I'd lay there, hair sticky, waiting for its swaying arms to brush a cool breeze over me. Watching sunlight glimmer like honey drops between its rustling leaves, I felt happy.

When it rained lightly in autumn, I'd sit and listen to raindrops pelt against the pavement, staying dry under its canopy. Then, I'd pour out my heart and confide in God. I found shelter under its shade.

God is our shade and shelter. God watches over you and me.

No matter how noisy the demands of the day get or how loud the voices of our inner critics clamor, there is a place where we are known. Loved. Accepted.

There is a place where we are *welcomed*. Deep in your heart, where God has made you His home, He assures you—*Rest in my shelter. I will be your shade.*

Shelter

Living in a rushing world that pushes us to be better and do more faster, we end up living in the noise of *not enough*. Our life becomes a treadmill of constant activity, striving to make our place in this world. Running on optimal speed, we feel empty. Always doing. No space to relax and just be.

Where do we belong? Do we belong? That bar of acceptance is always changing. The pressure drives us to maximize every opportunity, in fear of missing out. We might be busier, but it doesn't lead us to the shelter we truly long for. *Love. Joy. Peace. Purpose.*

Making space to rest and refresh returns our sanity. We can feel again and be inspired. We can find shelter from the world's noise. *We can nurture our God-given dreams to grow.*

Is there a growing desire or idea God's inviting you to nurture that would give you joy, peace, or purpose today? Has that dream stalled? The answer to getting unstuck isn't found in achieving or solving some *thing*. God's dream always calls us to go on a *journey with Him.*

Step away from busyness and step onto the journey to nurture your soul. Instead of relying on your own strength, *God can give you shelter and rest, so your dreams can take flight again.*

READ GOD'S STORY

If a dream has stalled or you're wondering how to encourage your heart, see the table set for you today. Feel Jesus gently fold his hand into yours, prompting you to stay and rest through the words of the Psalmist David:

> *"I will lift up my eyes to the mountains;*
> *From where shall my help come?*
> *My help comes from the Lord...*

The Lord watches over you—
the Lord is your shade at your right hand;
The sun will not smite you by day, Nor the moon by night."

PSALM 121:1–2, 5–6

"When my heart is faint;
Lead me to the rock that is higher than I.
For you have been my refuge, a strong tower…
Let me take shelter in the shadow of your wings."

PSALM 61:2–4

Hear God's quiet invitation to be your shelter. Jesus wants to share everything with you.

✏ God's Whispers to You

Beloved,
You don't have to work so hard to belong.
Rest in my love.
I am watching over you. Continually.

Your every dream stalled,
I will nurture to unlock everything beautiful
in your heart with me.

Let me be your shade. Rest and refresh.
I will be your shelter. Today.

✏ A Prayer for Today: When You Need Shelter

"You are my shelter and my shield; I put my hope in your word."

PSALM 119:114

Dear Jesus,
I run to you. You are my shelter.

I choose to step away
from busyness and striving—
to unlock my heart with you instead.

Guide me to create new rhythms
to nurture my heart to rest
and grow in trusting you.
I love you.
Amen.

Give Yourself Permission: Prioritize restarting your dreams. Guard your heart against critical people and invest in friends who encourage you. Guard your time. Refill your energy by doing things you enjoy and inspire you (a little every day or weekly break) instead of letting busyness and other people's priorities drain you.

REFLECT ON YOUR STORY

1. *What interests has God given you as shelter from the stress of this world?*

2. *What are things you can do to get inspired and nurture your passion?*

3. *What One Word in today's Psalms speaks to you?*

PRAY & REST

A SIMPLE PRACTICE: CONTEMPLATIVE PRAYER—THE PRAYER OF REST

Today, we practice *Contemplative Prayer*. We use our hearts to enter into *silence*, to *listen* and *experience* the presence of God. It's like leaning into a quiet embrace. Words aren't needed. Madame Guyon beautifully points us to: "Rest in God's love...Give your most intense attention to His still, small voice." Richard Foster calls it the "Prayer of Rest," defining it as "a loving attentiveness...more an experience of the heart than of the head."

Pray now by resting in silence with God. Use the One Word Prayer, *SHELTER*, as a focus. When your thoughts wander, gently return to your One Word. You may or may not hear God speak, or feel anything. That's okay. Just be with God.

Jesus, after resting in silence, this is how I feel...this is what I heard...

TODAY'S BELOVED CHALLENGE

Enjoy Looking at a Beautiful Tree
Rest under its shade,
walk, or bike where trees will refresh you.

Return to a peaceful place with the One who shelters you.

SOUL CARE
TRAIL
NOTES

Simply Looking at Trees Reduces Your Stress Levels

There is something about a tree that brings God's whispers to the surface. We feel refreshed. Research confirms that simply looking at trees helps people become less stressed, and the effect increases the more trees are visible. The greater the amount of tree density people viewed, the greater the stress reduction.

So a powerful way to significantly reduce the amount of stress in your life and recover better from daily stress is by simply taking a walk down a tree-lined street. Or better yet, take a stroll in the park. One Glasgow University study even found that the positive effect of walking, biking, or running on grass or a trail for people suffering from depression and anxiety was *twice as good* as a trip to the gym for mental well-being!

PART FOUR

Healing as the Beloved

Turn Brokenness into Beauty:
Experience a Deeper Intimacy with Jesus

As your heart opens up to dream again,
the wounds that once hurt you may still hold you back.

It is time to go on the intimate journey of healing with God.

Jesus whispers,
I am making all things new.
I will heal your brokenness into beauty.

This next collection of devotionals guides you
to meet with Jesus in his most vulnerable moments
before he was betrayed.

Each day's reflection invites you
to meet with Jesus in his most vulnerable moments.
To begin healing the feelings of fear, shame, and rejection
in the loving presence of your Savior.

"See, I am doing something new. Now it springs forth…
Will you not be aware of it? I will make a way in the
wilderness and rivers in the desert."   ISAIAH 43:19

Remember

Broken-Hearted Healing

Let me love you. My love will heal you.

You don't have to be unbroken to be loved.
Just look down at the hand holding yours.

Jesus tenderly whispers,
You are my forever home.
Let me love you. My love will heal you.
Today.

"The Lord is near to the brokenhearted
And saves those who are crushed in spirit…
He heals the brokenhearted and binds up their wounds."

PSALM 34:18, 147:3

"Earth has no sorrow that Heaven cannot heal."

THOMAS MOORE

She looked cute as a button. She sparkled with her brown eyes, a dimpled smile, and strands of chestnut hair pulled up in a ponytail that fringed her sweet face.

"She's five," my friend Amy★ whispered back when I'd silently mouthed, *How old is she?*

"You're so cute! You know that?" I playfully said to the little girl, stooping down to let out a giggle to match hers.

She was bashful but not shy. I knew that behind her sunshine laugh lay a broken heart. You see, my friend Amy was a foster parent, and this little girl with her was a foster child with a painful past.

"What is your name?" I asked. She turned to tell me. "Oh, what a beautiful name." I cooed. She was Special Little Girl. "I love your pink cardigan. And look at your shoes. Mary Janes in pink glitter! Is pink your favorite color?" She nodded.

"We went shopping. She picked out her own clothes," Amy chimes in.

"Well, you did a great job! You look beautiful," I said. Special Little Girl beamed with pride.

I found out later that when her mother visited and saw Special Little Girl dressed in her new outfit, she said, "You look stupid." The courts had removed her from her mother. Her father was no better. She wasn't safe with them.

I asked Special Little Girl if I could give her a hug, and she nodded yes. And because I didn't know when I'd see her next

---

★ Her real name has been changed for privacy.

(you never know how long a foster child stays), I looked deep into her eyes and told her as tenderly as I could:

Jesus loves you very much, sweetheart. You are a very special little girl. Don't you ever forget that. You are special. She smiled.

Healing

I couldn't stop thinking of Special Little Girl when I got home. I cried because she was so young. I cried because it broke my heart imagining her alone in this world. Without a home. Without someone to turn to and call her cherished.

I cried because there's a part of me learning to come home, too, and there are places in me still needing healing. Because, like Special Little Girl, we're all still on our way coming home to God's love.

Are there parts of your heart in need of God's healing as well? Although all looks well on the outside, are there wounds still stinging from what was said or what has happened to you? We all carry pain from living in a broken world.

Jesus is here to assure us—*I remember you. My love will heal you.*

Deep inside, we all long to belong to someone. Someone kind and loving, Gentle. Faithful. No matter what has happened, you were meant to be loved. *Cherished and remembered.* Every broken part of your story can be healed, because it never has to be hidden, but instead loved back to life.

Jesus tells us he is that Someone, lovingly whispering your name—*I remember you, Beloved.*

READ GOD'S STORY

Maybe on the night before he died, Jesus looked into the eyes of his friends and saw the special little girls and boys in each of them. Jesus knew each of their stories, and Jesus knows yours and mine.

Jesus knew his disciples would be scared and confused, but he also knew his love would heal their broken hearts. So he spent his last moments washing their feet, to rest at a table together and share a meal. Jesus made an oath. He would never leave them. He would love them to the end.

> *"Jesus knew that the time had come*
> *for him to leave this world and go back to the Father.*
> *Having loved his own who were in the world,*
> *He loved them to the end."* JOHN 13:1

Jesus made *a new promise* to be our forever home—by giving up his body and life. Jesus whispered:

> *Whenever you eat this bread . . . of brokenness . . .*
> *Whenever you drink this cup . . . of life pouring out . . .*
> *Remember me. Because I'm remembering you.*

Close your eyes. Imagine Jesus now—standing in the midst of your worries and preoccupation—quietly rolling up his sleeves, kneeling and looking into your eyes. See him reaching out his hand, his fingers relaxed, ready to wash your feet, if you'd let him.

He wants to heal your heart with his love. He's brought a warm basin of water. You can relax and rest. You are safe with him.

See the dream he carried in his heart onto the cross—to love, hold, and heal you—coming true in you today. Reflect on the Psalmist David's words as prayer:

> *"I sought the Lord, and He answered me,*
> *And delivered me from all my fears.*

They looked to Him and were radiant,
And their faces will never be ashamed…

The Lord is near to the brokenhearted
And saves those who are crushed in spirit."

PSALM 34:4–5, 18

"He heals the brokenhearted
and binds up their wounds."

PSALM 147:3

Remember. Jesus whispers love to you.

✑ God's Whispers to You

Beloved,
Remember how far I'd go, just to be with you.
I promise. I'm never going to leave you orphaned.

You are my forever home.
I'll journey with you. Every day. All the way.

Let go of whatever you're holding on to.
Let me hold on to you instead.

Let me love you. My love will heal you.
Today.

✑ A Prayer for Today: When You Need God's Healing

The Lord is near to the brokenhearted
And saves those who are crushed in spirit.

*"He heals the brokenhearted and binds up their
wounds."*   PSALM 34:18, 147:3

Lord Jesus,
You feel my heartache.
You know my story and my pain.

Give me courage to take steps to heal today.
Guide me on this journey of healing.
I'm willing because you love me.
You'll never leave me.

Walk with me.
Just like you promised.
I'm holding on to you. I need you.
Thank you for suffering, so you can love me forever.
Today.
Amen.

You don't have to be unbroken to be loved. You are special
to Jesus.

Give Yourself Permission: Open up. Take steps to heal.
Investigate your stress, anxiety, or wounded spirit. Be
curious about other people's stories. Ask questions. Be
curious about your own story. Find a trusted confidant
or therapist to help you explore the mysteries of your
story and your healing.

REFLECT ON YOUR STORY

1. *What is Jesus whispering to you to remember about yourself or your*
   story?

2. *If you could experience healing without fear of others judging you, what would it be?*

3. *What One Word speaks to you in today's beautiful passages of Scripture?*

PRAY & REST

A SIMPLE PRACTICE: A LETTER TO YOUR YOUNGER SELF

Corrie ten Boom, a Dutch Christian imprisoned for helping Jews escape the Nazis, never erased her memories. She quoted her father in *The Hiding Place*: " 'Do you know what hurts so very much? It's love. Love is the strongest force in the world, and when it is blocked that means pain... We can kill the love so that it stops hurting. But then of course part of us dies, too. Or... we can ask God to open up another route for that love to travel.' " Let's open a new route by healing our memories with God in prayer.

For today's prayer, write a letter to your younger self. *What would you say to your younger self based on what you know now? At what point in life would you speak to her?* Let the little girl in you be present with Jesus now.

Dear _____, *Age:* _____

TODAY'S BELOVED CHALLENGE

Enjoy Doodling or Coloring

Pull out your colored pencils or crayons.
Art is therapy for the soul. Destress. Relax.

"Art washes from the soul the dust of everyday life" (Pablo Picasso). Make space to nurture the little girl in you who dreams. Do an art project.

SOUL CARE TRAIL NOTES

Coloring Calms and Destresses

Coloring is a fun and creative way to decompress from the stress of the day and reconnect with the little girl in you. Choosing colors and making repetitive, small movements calms the part of the brain that stresses out (it's called the amygdala).

Coloring elicits a relaxation and a meditation-like response by helping you focus on the moment, practice mindfulness, and temporarily push aside worries. Psychologist Gloria Martinez says that coloring "brings out our imagination and takes us back to our childhood."

Stay

Presence Is Healing

Stay and let me hold you today.

When you wonder will anyone stay,
Jesus whispers—
Don't be afraid.
I call you by name. I call you mine.

Stay and let me hold you today.
I am that Someone. I will stay.

"Do not fear, for I have redeemed you;
I have called you by name; you are mine." ISAIAH 43:1

※ ※ ※

"The wound is the place where the light enters you."

During my season recovering from panic attacks triggered by emotional posttraumatic stress from childhood, I became very sensitive to loud music.

Then, after a breakthrough in therapy, on the other side of my healing and my nervous system was happy again, I wanted to see Gungor in concert. They were playing in San Francisco. So I texted our babysitter and found myself standing in a concert hall next to Eric on one side and two twenty-something girls with summer in their eyes on the other. We had an hour left before the curtains lifted.

I found out both girls were seminary students. "So what're you studying? What's next?" You might think people who look happy and perfect wouldn't have hard stories to share. But they do.

The blue-eyed, blond-haired girl told me, half-yelling across the drone of concertgoers, "I'm not really sure what God wants me to do. I've told Him I'll do whatever he wants me to do."

She paused. *"But I feel like I've been wandering."* Blue-Eyed Girl told me she'd been hurt. She'd run into dead ends when she thought God had been opening doors. All of a sudden, it felt like there was no one else in the room. *Except her unspoken story and me.*

The pre-PTSD me would have given her some cheerful advice. Safe words. But now I see everything differently. When the world we live in doesn't match the dreams God put on our hearts, don't we all feel a little lost?

When we step out and try to be ourselves—and offer

something authentic, only to discover someone doesn't think it's good enough—don't we all wonder who would stay? And when we have to face something hard, but we don't know how long the journey will take and we want to give up—but we can't go back, either—don't we wonder why God is silent?

We ask God, *Is there any other way?*

Any Other Way

These were the words Jesus whispered in a garden one night in Gethsemane into thick silence. Wave upon wave of questions poured out of him. The dilemma of turning left or right was both as painful as it was unwanted. "Is there any other way?" Jesus asked.

Jesus could have chosen to pray by himself and hide this inner struggle. Jesus often prayed alone. Yet on the worst night of his life, Jesus tells us he needed someone to hold on to the hard moment with him.

Jesus needed someone to stay.

Jesus didn't have a timetable to know how long the journey of the cross would take. How long the beatings would last. How long he'd have to drag the cross inch by inch, with lashes bleeding cut deep in his back. He didn't know how he would feel yanked around in chains, from one place to another, in sleep deprivation.

Jesus had never, ever, experienced the feel of spit on his face while he shivered in the cold alone. *The overwhelming anxiety of the unknown, but the certain pain and fear of what was to come, brought Jesus to his knees.* Right to where you and I sometimes have to go, when we don't know what to do.

Overwhelmed, Jesus turned to those closest to him. Jesus became vulnerable and let his disciples see him, as desperation filled the pit of his stomach.

READ GOD'S STORY

Enter this private moment with Jesus now, as he whispers what he said that night to you. Jesus confided in his closest friends, as he stumbled right up to the edge of himself.

"Then he said to [Peter, James and John]—
'My soul is overwhelmed with sorrow to the point of death.
Stay here... with me.'

Going a little farther, he fell with his face to the ground and prayed,
'My Father, if there is any way, get me out of this.' "

MATTHEW 26:38–39

Jesus asked someone to stay with him that night. ***Jesus needed someone to stay.***

The Scriptures tell us Jesus was so overwhelmed with anguish that his sweat fell like drops of blood. Could Jesus have been experiencing panic attacks? If you've ever had one, you might never see that night in Gethsemane the same way again. This was how Jesus spent his final moments of solitude.

"*Stay here... with me,*" he said. Jesus is intimately familiar with the pain of a journey unresolved—right in the middle of it.

Yet, unlike me, Jesus did not yield to temptation. *Jesus, instead, yielded to the journey.* Willingly. Lovingly. Completely. For you. For me.

🖋 *God's Whispers to You*

Beloved,
I've wandered willingly into darkness one night long ago
So you don't have to walk alone anymore.

When you wonder if anyone will stay,
don't be afraid. I've redeemed you.
I call you by name. I call you mine.

Stay and let me hold you today.
I am that Someone. I will stay.

We don't have to be alone anymore—even when we fail to yield. Especially in the moments when we want to, but we don't know how. Jesus suffered for us, so that he can stay with us, in the middle of it all. God's presence is healing.

In our wandering, we are never truly lost. Having someone to hold on to changes everything. Having someone love you in the waiting—in the suffering—*changes you.* When someone stays with us, we become the Beloved.

Love heals.

The Best Gift

I turned to Blue-Eyed Girl and said, "You know, I think we're all wanderers in this life. We're all on a journey. Maybe wandering is living out faith. *Maybe the best gift we can offer* to others wandering in this world without hope is *to walk as a wanderer with them—with hope.* Maybe being willing to wander with Jesus is one of the sweetest gifts we surrender to him."

The best gift we can offer each another is our presence. Blue-Eyed Girl hugged me. "Thank you," she said, smiling and squeezing my hand.

✏ *A Prayer for Today:*
When You Need Someone to Stay

"Do not fear, for I have redeemed you;
I have called you by name; you are mine."　　ISAIAH 43:1

Dear Jesus,
I need someone. Stay with me.
You understand my fears and my sorrow.

Love me. Heal me.
Take care of me.
Guide me to the other side of my healing.

Strengthen me with your love.
Give me courage to yield to the journey with you,
to say as you did—not what I want. But what you want.

Thank you for all you suffered for me.
Amen.

Give Yourself Permission: Honor your Gethsemane moment. Grieve what's hard. Don't suffer alone. Confide in someone to stay with you in a hard moment. Begin with Jesus. Then share with a friend or two as Jesus did. Let love heal your heart.

REFLECT ON YOUR STORY

1. *What is your Gethsemane moment?*

2. *What are times you felt lost, alone or wandering?*

3. *Do you find it easy or difficult to confide in others about yourself? Why? How you can let someone into your hard moments?*

4. *What One Word speaks to you today?*

PRAY & REST

A SIMPLE PRACTICE: KNEELING IN PRAYER

Let's kneel in prayer. Experience intimate prayer as Jesus did, kneeling as a child longs for his father's comfort and nearness. Jesus poured out his heart honestly, expressing his feelings through his body in the vulnerable posture of a child. We can, too. "Do you wish to rise?" St. Augustine asked. "Begin by descending. You plan a tower that will pierce the clouds? Lay first the foundation of humility."

Kneel where you are at. Imagine Jesus next to you (he is), with tenderness for you. Be still. Breathe. Rest in his presence. Let today's One Word Prayer, *STAY,* invite you to confide and pray. Afterward, share: *Jesus, this is how I felt kneeling to pray . . .*

TODAY'S BELOVED CHALLENGE

Aromatherapy
Enjoy the Aroma of Your Favorite Essential Oil
Energize and restore calm to your body and spirit.

Explore which scents feel nurturing and healing to your soul.

SOUL CARE TRAIL NOTES

Benefits of Aromatherapy

Our feelings are connected to our body's response. When we feel overwhelmed, our God-designed nervous system alerts us with fast heartbeats, triggering stress, anxiety, and feelings of depression. Just as Jesus' loving presence calms our spirit, natural God-given scents also signal calm to our nervous system.

Our sense of smell is linked to the "feeling" part of our brains. Science shows that aromas powerfully affect our emotional well-being. A study of female nursing students found that the fragrance of lavender effectively improved depression and insomnia. A Mayo Clinic research found that smelling orange oil for five minutes reduced stress and anxiety responses in vital symptoms after participants took a test. Peppermint soothes headaches, boosting memory, while lemon energizes. What calms you is unique to each person, so experiment with various scents.

Need Someone

Healing Shame

We all need someone. Hold on to me.

When the weight of the journey feels heavy,
and you feel all alone,
Jesus whispers—
You don't have to be unbroken to be loved.
We all need someone.
Come. Hold on to me.

"Blessed are those whose strength is in you,
whose hearts are set on pilgrimage.
When they walk through the Valley of Weeping,
it will become a place of refreshing springs."

PSALM 84:5–6

> "I'm writing this in part to tell you that if you ever won-
> der what you've done in your life, you have been God's
> grace to me."   MARILYNNE ROBINSON

We all need someone.

This is a beautiful, lonely, hard, and easy truth. Beautiful if you have someone. Lonely if you don't. Hard for the times you'd rather not need. Easy for the times when someone you need needs you, too.

When my first book was published, you might have seen me with my loving husband, Eric, and two beautiful kids, Josh and Caleb, and you might have thought I ought to have been so happy.

I was. But I want to confide in you. I want to tell you that the journey to really becoming the Beloved, to truly find-ing your voice, may inevitably lead you back to parts of your story—people, experiences, conversations, or situations—you'd rather avoid. That are painful but honest. You may be tempted to choose safety. To stay quiet and hide, rather than be vulner-able and real.

You may have to make some hard decisions where there are no certain outcomes. You may have to take up a cross that's hard to bear. *Maybe like me, in order to follow God where he wants to take you, you will need to go through uncertainty. Maybe even loss.*

Even though you know God is with you and faith will get you through, you cannot avoid the hardness of the journey. And even though there is much to be thankful for—and you're grateful for how God walks with you—you cannot deny the weight of the cross on your shoulders.

The hardness of the journey doesn't mean you're on the wrong path.

Who Are We?

God calls you to dare to experience being His Beloved. As is. Today. To step out and make choices you've never made before. To say no, when it's more comfortable to say yes. To say yes today, rather than waiting to be better tomorrow.

It's hard. Who are we to call ourselves Beloved—in light of our brokenness?

It's the same question launched at Jesus by the Roman soldiers who put a staff in his hand to mock him as king, crushed a crown of thorns onto his head, and whipped him, then threw him out of the praetorium.

The praetorium was the governor's hall, where Pontius Pilate issued Jesus the death sentence, where the soldiers assaulted Jesus emotionally, hurling wounding words targeted to bring shame and humiliation. It wasn't enough to break his body. They wanted to break his heart and his spirit with their words. (See Matthew 27:26–31.)

They mocked him—*Who are you to call yourself a king?* After this abuse occurred in secrecy, Jesus took his steps through the very public streets of Via Dolorosa. In front of everyone.

> "When they led Him away, they seized a man, Simon of Cyrene, coming in from the country, and placed on him the cross to carry behind Jesus."   LUKE 23:26

It's likely that following his beating, Jesus could not physically carry the cross all the way to Calvary. *Jesus needed someone.*

In that moment, a man whose journey somehow crossed Jesus' path was pulled in to help him. We don't know if Simon even knew who Jesus was. Did they exchange even a single word? It's unknown. All we do know is that an ordinary person helped the Savior. Through one simple, understated act, a person became part of the journey with Jesus.

It's okay to need someone. When the cross is too heavy to carry—but we still want to be faithful to see the journey through—*we should not be ashamed to need someone. It isn't shameful to be broken—because we are still, and always, beloved.*

READ GOD'S STORY

Is Jesus calling you to step forward on a journey that feels uncertain and daunting? Don't be ashamed at the weight of that cross. Or what others might say about you. Listen to Jesus assure you that he carries your emotional wounds, so that you can be healed of all shame today:

> "One look at him and people turned away.
> We looked down on him, thought he was scum.
>
> But the fact is, it was our pains he carried—
> our disfigurements, all the things wrong with us.
>
> We thought he brought it on himself,
> that God was punishing him for his own failures.
>
> But it was our sins that did that to him,
> that ripped and tore and crushed him—our sins!
> He took the punishment, and that made us whole.
>
> Surely our grief he himself bore,
> and our sorrows he carried…
> and by his wounds we are healed."   ISAIAH 53:3–5

Experiencing shame won't keep Jesus from you. He wraps his healing love around you. Keep stepping forward.

Think of Jesus. Imagine how his steps on the Via Dolorosa were soaked in shame and emotional anguish amid the sea of wounding voices. Then think of Simon who walked alongside him, carrying the cross for him.

Jesus needed someone. He doesn't want you to journey alone either.

✑ God's Whispers to You

Beloved,
When the weight of the journey feels heavy,
and you feel all alone, come to me.

You don't have to be unbroken to be loved.
You don't have to feel ashamed.
We all need someone. Just hold on to me.

I've felt every sting of the hurtful words hurled at you,
as I walked the broken road long ago
and even now, as I walk it again with you.

Now let me place someone on your path.
To carry your cross with you.

It's okay to need someone.
Let me love you through a friend.

✍ *A Prayer for Today*: *When You Need Someone*

*"Blessed are those whose strength is in you,
whose hearts are set on pilgrimage.
When they walk through the Valley of Weeping,
it will become a place of refreshing springs."*

PSALM 84:5–6

*Dear Jesus,
Thank you for walking the lonely, broken road,
so I don't have to walk alone anymore.*

*I need someone. I need you.
Heal my feelings of shame.*

*Give me courage to need others.
To share my burdens. To trust again.*

*Transform my brokenness to become a doorway of your love
to listen and be someone's friend. Just like you.*

*Thank you. Your love is amazing.
You are my everything. I love you.
Amen.*

Give Yourself Permission: Prioritize nurturing one-on-one friendships to help you carry the burden. Break the secrecy of shame and heal by sharing the words or actions that have hurt you. Express your needs. Practice receiving. Let go of toxic relationships that emotionally wound you. Enforce firm boundaries.

REFLECT ON YOUR STORY

1. *How is God encouraging you to open up and share your heart with others?*

2. *How do you relate to the word "shame"? What areas are you vulnerable to experiencing feelings of shame?*

3. *As you read about the different ways Jesus experienced shame, what spoke personally to you? How did you feel imagining Jesus suffering?*

4. *What One Word speaks to you in today's powerful Scriptures?*

PRAY & REST

A SIMPLE PRACTICE: A CANDLELIT PRAYER

St. Francis of Assisi asked, "Dear Brother, go to Sister Claire and tell her on my behalf to pray to God...that he may show me what is best. Then go to Brother Silvester and tell him the same thing." Who are the Simons in your life? Who has been there for you, prayed for you? Picture them. What they said. What they did.

For today's prayer, light a candle to express the light they have been for you. Think of them. Thank God for them. Ask God to bless and protect them. Write a note to that friend who has helped you climb the hill of life.

Jesus, thank you for...

TODAY'S BELOVED CHALLENGE

Schedule Coffee with a Friend

Talk about how you're feeling, not just what you're doing. Friendship heals the soul.

None of us can make it through this life alone. Life is imperfect. Even Jesus journeyed with trusted friends. Be vulnerable. It's healing to journey together.

SOUL CARE TRAIL NOTES

Talking About Your Feelings Is Healing

Just as Jesus named his emotions by sharing "my soul is overwhelmed with sorrow" (Matthew 26:38), we can feel better by verbalizing our negative feelings. A brain-imaging study by UCLA psychologists revealed that simply putting words to our feelings reduces the level of emotional pain we experience.

Participants were asked to view images of people expressing emotions like anger and sadness. As they did, researchers saw brain activity in the amygdala (the area that triggers stress anxiety in the nervous system) fire up like crazy. But when people *simply labeled the emotions* they observed, it reduced the brain's emotional activity, restoring calm.

Don't hide your negative feelings to feel better or force yourself to move past them. Instead, talk about your feelings, and you'll curiously feel better!

DAY 24

⁂ ⁂ ⁂

Make a Way

Healing the Past

Lean into me. I will make a way for you.

Lean into me. I will make a way for you.
There is no place we can find ourselves,
where Jesus will not go.

Jesus assures us—
I am doing something new.
Love makes a way.
Lean in. I will make a way for you.

"See, I am doing something new.
Now it springs forth. Will you not be aware of it?
I will make a way in the wilderness and rivers
in the desert."   ISAIAH 43:19

"The longing itself is evidence that what you are longing
for really exists." KAREN BLIXEN

Something happens when you find yourself lying on your bed
unable to fall asleep. Not just for one or two nights. Sometimes, life enters seasons of uncertainty and trials that keep you
awake.

You feel restless and search your heart for glimmers of what
once made you feel alive. Young and innocent. Refreshed.

Jesus understands and sees that longing in us—*to find a way,
to feel safe and held again.* As sunlight first warms you in the
morning, Jesus draws near to whisper:

I am here.

Making a way. For you. With you.

And you begin to cry. Because you miss the nearness of
God's tender touch.

I found myself in too many restless, sleepless nights, for a
long season to heal and find God's whispers of rest to revitalize
my soul. But as I lay there, I found in that pit of darkness *something beautiful and true.*

I found I could remember God's goodness. And because it
told me that it was in me once, that goodness had to still be in
me now. In that moment, I chose to believe that remembrance
of goodness was my faith, still breathing in me.

The fact that I longed for goodness and hungered for it told
me that nothing—not even my wounded self—could rob me
of those memories. That Goodness had a name. *It was God's
Holy Spirit, alive in me. And He is also alive in you today.*

When you feel wounded and God seems far away, even the
remembrance of God's goodness is evidence of his Holy Spirit
moving in your heart.

"Your name, even your memory, is the desire of our souls.
At night my soul longs for you.
Indeed, my spirit within me seeks you diligently".

ISAIAH 26:8–9

That stirring comes from Jesus. Jesus understands how *being wounded once led him to remember all that captured his heart one dark day.*

A Deeper Wounding

One of the darkest moments Jesus faced are found in *three words*—spoken after Pilate washed his hands, released Barabbas, and had Jesus flogged with a cat-o'-nine-tails, a whip the Romans used.

"My friend, Kevin Marks, in writing his meditations for *Stations of the Cross*, tell us—"

"Historians tell us the whip was divided into several strips, each containing shards of broken pottery at their ends, enabling them to cut skin and tear flesh from bone. Most Roman prisoners didn't live through these beatings due to shock and loss of blood. Third-century historian Eusebius described the process in grotesque detail: 'The sufferer's veins were laid bare, and the very muscles, sinews, and bowels of the victim were open to exposure.'"

Although crippled by such physical torture, Jesus, who somehow survived, had to endure *a deeper wounding—which is found in three words* written at the close of this scene.

"Then he released Barabbas to them.
But he had Jesus flogged,
*and **handed him over** to be crucified."*   MATTHEW 27:26

Handed. Him. Over.
Jesus was handed over. I can hear Jesus crying, not out of fear but out of physical and emotional pain. He was abandoned.

Completely given up by everyone. Life for Jesus would never be without the scars of betrayal. His story could never be untainted by betrayal, loneliness, and rejection.

But Jesus chose it all, because behind the brokenness, he carried the memories of why he was willing to live out this story that was rapidly unraveling.

Jesus carried live, beautiful memories of—

How he made you in the secret place.
The warmth of your first breath caressing his heart.
The sunshine of your smile.

Jesus was healing the past by enduring all the brokenness and devastation his body and soul could carry. *Because in his wounding, Jesus can heal us today.*

There is no place we can find ourselves where Jesus will not go. Jesus makes his home in us. As is. His love makes a way. God is making a way. In you. For you.

☞ *God's Whispers to You*

Beloved,
There is no place you'll find yourself,
where I will not go with you.

When you wonder what lies ahead,
you can rest.

Even in your wounded-ness,
I will never leave you.

I am doing something new.
Love makes a way.
Lean into me. I will make a way for you.

Jesus loves you. And me. Passionately. Irrevocably. Shamelessly and completely.

When I realized life was never going to be the same for me again, I stopped wishing to be rescued. I began to desperately *pray for courage to heal instead.* To lean in. To move toward the longing I still carried for goodness. For beauty. For God.

That desire for goodness became my silent prayer. Like a flickering candle that somehow stays lit through the night, God made a way to heal my heart. This book of whispers of rest you're holding? It was the journey of love God led me on—and now we can sojourn together.

No matter how whisper thin, imperfect, or insignificant your movements forward may feel, God is making a way for you. Today. He's calling you to go *no farther than just the one step in front of you.*

Jesus puts his hand in yours, to draw you toward him. Jesus surrendered to being handed over—even until his last breath— *so he can make a way for you today.* So Jesus can carry you. *All the way.*

No matter where the journey of life takes you, God's love is strong enough to heal your past, so you can rewrite your story today as His Beloved.

Don't let anyone or the hardness of the journey convince you otherwise. *Lean in. To Jesus. Be the Beloved.*

✑ *A Prayer for Today:* *Trust God to Make a Way for You*

"See, I am doing something new.
Now it springs forth. Will you not be aware of it?
I will make a way in the wilderness and rivers in the
desert."   ISAIAH 43:19

Dear Jesus,
Give me courage to lean in. To you.
To take just the one step you're inviting me to take. Today.
To trust you'll make a roadway in the wilderness.
Even rivers in the desert.

Even though I can't see the way ahead,
I surrender myself to your love.

Because you are the Way.
You are my Way.
In this very moment. Today.

Thank you for loving me as your heart and body broke.
Thank you for your Holy Spirit who heals me,
moves and empowers me to walk and pray.
I love you. I am yours today. Always.
Amen.

Tomorrow can be different. God will make a way when there seems to be no way.

Give Yourself Permission: Take just one step in front of you. Trust God will show you the next step at the moment you need it.

REFLECT ON YOUR STORY

1. *What is one thing God is inviting you to lean into today with Him?*

2. *How is God asking you to make different choices from the past? What is the "roadway" in the wilderness for you? What are the "rivers" in the desert he is providing for you?*

3. *How are wounds from the past affecting your well-being, confidence, decision making, and relationships today? How can you take steps to heal those wounds?*

4. *What One Word speaks to you today?*

PRAY & REST

A SIMPLE PRACTICE: DAILY EXAMEN PRAYER—CUDDLE UP TO JESUS

St. Ignatius of Loyola encouraged people to talk to Jesus as a friend by praying the Daily Examen. *The Daily Examen is a cozy conversation with Jesus at the end of the day.* You review the day at night with your confidant Jesus—by walking through events, examining your feelings, taking note of his presence—and ask for guidance, forgiveness, or whatever you need.

The Daily Examen is one of my favorite ways to cuddle up to Jesus in the details of daily life. St. Ignatius taught it to Jesuits priests so they'd experience God's love. It's been practiced for hundreds of years. I know you'll enjoy it too.

Inspired by today's One Word Prayer, *MAKE A WAY,* use the five prompts below to pray the Daily Examen, and allow God to have His way in you now.

The Daily Examen Prayer

1. Gratitude. *I'm grateful I saw you in these moments today . . .*

2. Be Aware of God's Presence. *I felt you close to me as I saw, thought, or realized . . .*

3. Share Your Emotions. *Today, I felt this when that happened . . .*

4. Focus on One Event to Ask God Anything. *I need your light, wisdom or_____ in this situation or decision today . . .*

5. Look Toward Tomorrow. *I lift this up to you for tomorrow. I need hope and help in . . .*

TODAY'S BELOVED CHALLENGE

Take a Thirty-Minute Nap

Revitalize, reenergize, and destress.

Rejuvenate your body and soul with rest. As you do, you're putting God's love for you into action, coming alive in a new way of living.

SOUL CARE TRAIL NOTES

Taking a Nap Is Healing

Reviewing the day with Jesus brings rest, preparing us for sleep. But during our Gethsemane moments, sleep can be troubled. We need seven to nine hours of sleep a night. Research shows lack of sleep affects our mood, heightening irritability, anxiety, and depression. Taking a nap makes a difference.

Research also shows a thirty-minute nap reduces stress and boosts the immune system, reversing the effects of occasional sleep deprivation. Participants restricted to sleeping only two hours showed elevated stress hormones and a decrease in immunity proteins. But after a nap, all markers returned to normal.

A nap improves mood and boosts memory, performance, and attention. So on demanding days, take a nap. Rejuvenate yourself with the healing benefits of rest.

DAY 25

Brokenness

Healing Beauty

Come into my arms. I will heal your brokenness into beauty.

·Everything broken leads us
to everything beautiful.

Because in everything broken,
there stands Jesus.

He whispers—
I will heal your brokenness into beauty.
I love you.

"We are more than conquerors through him who loved us.
I am convinced that nothing can ever separate us from
God's love." ROMANS 8:37–39

✿ ✿ ✿

"You see, there are two very different types of hope in this world. One is hoping for something, and the other is hoping in someone."
                                                    PETE WILSON

I don't want to be one of those people.

Someone who is afraid. Someone who can't deal with hard things and fails to overcome. Yet, here I was, unable to deny that—*I was afraid*. I was discouraged. What I was terrified to face is this: *I couldn't make my place in this world*.

I couldn't do the things I once did, and I was afraid that friends, family, colleagues, and readers would walk away and shake their heads. I'd be all alone. These were the words I spoke into the dark, walking through my season healing from anxiety.

You would've never known I truly felt this way. All my life, I've nurtured a determination to never come close to this place of aloneness. *I am a child of light. Why would I want to face into darkness?*

I believed that faith was relegated to creating a safe place for myself in this world and for the ones I love—to love Jesus by serving and loving others. Yet, I never imagined that *faith in Jesus is exactly what it takes to enter* into *a place of truth and vulnerability—a place of empty. Brokenness.*

But it was time for deeper intimacy. He didn't want me to do anything for him. *Jesus wanted to love me deeper.* Jesus knew I was strong enough to finally face the part of me he wanted to love back to life: my wounded self.

How about you? Could you or someone you love be standing at the doorway of something that feels hard, that renders you unable to do as you've always done? Are you feeling discouraged and alone?

You haven't failed in your faith. *Jesus wants to love you deeper.*

Jesus knows when you find ourselves in a valley, you are no longer able to use the strength and hope you've always drawn from. Jesus will help and heal you with his love.

Jesus knows because he's been there himself. This place of alone. *This place of empty.*

Heartsick

In the Garden of Gethsemane, we find Jesus:

> *"Being in agony... his sweat became like drops of blood, falling down upon the ground."* LUKE 22:44

Jesus escaped to a private place where he felt safe. It was there his disciple Matthew tells us, *"Jesus fell on His face and prayed, saying, 'My Father, if it is possible, let this cup pass from me'"* (Matthew 26:39).

The Gospel of Mark gives us a private glimpse into the Jesus we rarely talk about: *"He began to be very distressed and troubled."* Overwhelmed by anxiety, Jesus confides to Peter, James, and John, *"My soul is deeply grieved to the point of death"* (Mark 14:-33–34). Jesus is utterly heartsick, down where pain has never reached before.

Healing Beauty

Even though Jesus was in total control to become the scapegoat for sin, he cried out, *"Abba! Father! All things are possible for You; Remove this cup from Me."* (Mark 14:36).

If there was any other way out, he wished for it then. *But there wasn't any other way.* Jesus had to face the toughest journey head-on.

Jesus willingly placed himself in God's rescue plan, yet he

still stepped into the place of being utterly, forsakenly empty (see Philippians 2:5–8). We can imagine Jesus falling to the ground, choking back waves of tears, his body shaking, his chest hurting from the intensity of his emotions.

So whenever we ask, "Is there any beauty in brokenness?" Jesus points us to the healing beauty of his love for us that night in Gethsemane. *Yes. There is beauty in brokenness—because I am right there with you.*

READ GOD'S STORY

Draw near to Jesus to hear the most intimate words he once spoke in the dark.

"Yet not my will, but yours be done."   LUKE 22:42

Beloved,
You can accept this—because I know how it feels when
God's plan leads the world to see you as wounded. Broken.
I will give you the courage. You don't have to be strong. I will
be strong for you.

Jesus points us to the scene of his betrayal, when Peter tried to stop him from walking down the path of weakness:

Put the sword into the sheath; the cup which the Father
has given me, shall I not drink it?   JOHN 18:11

Beloved,
You can swallow this cup of brokenness—because I drank from
it myself. You can feel afraid with me. I will hold you and love
you through it.

In the garden of Gethsemane, Jesus said, "Not my will." Jesus had a will—*and it was contrary to God's will in that moment of suffering* (see Hebrews 5:7–10). This is comforting, because even as we take the cup of brokenness in our hands, we don't want it. *Jesus understands this place of painful tension.*

Unlike me, Jesus did not give in to his temptation to avoid the place of empty. He surrenders:

> *"Yet not my will, but yours be done."*　　　LUKE 22:42

In other words, absolutely nothing can separate God's love from us. *Not even brokenness.*

> *I am convinced that nothing can ever separate us from God's love.*
>
> *Neither death nor life, neither angels nor demons, neither the present nor the future, nor any powers, neither height nor depth, nor anything else in all creation, will be able to separate us from the love of God that is in Christ Jesus.*　　　ROMANS 8:37–39

☞ *God's Whispers to You*

Beloved,
Come here. Into my arms.
There is nothing—absolutely nothing—
that can tear me away from loving you.
You are safe. I am your forever place.

I will never be parted from you.
I will heal your brokenness into beauty,

because I am here loving you irrevocably.
You are my Beloved. Today. As is.

Are you finding yourself holding a cup you don't want to drink? You don't have to want the cup in order to take and drink it—*with Jesus.* Jesus folds your hand into his today.

✍ *A Prayer for Today:*
God Heals Brokenness into Beauty

"In all these things, we are more than conquerors through Him who loved us. I am convinced that nothing can ever separate us from God's love."

ROMANS 8:37–39

Dear Jesus,
Give me courage to drink the cup
that comes from letting you love me deeper.

Heal my brokenness into beauty.
This journey isn't one I would choose for myself,
so give me courage to share my broken moments
with friends, just like you did.

Thank you for being brave and beautiful,
baring your heart in your moment of greatest vulnerability.
I love you, Jesus.
Amen.

No matter what is hurt or broken—whether it's our childhood, a relationship, career, marriage, our children, health, finances, or ministry—our dreams or opportunities—your place of empty is never out of His reach. *Brokenness isn't the end of your story. God's love is.*

Everything broken leads us to everything beautiful. Because in everything broken, there stands Jesus. Healing you deeper with his love every day.

Give Yourself Permission: Surround yourself with beauty. Listen to beautiful music, see art, drive out to the ocean or a beautiful place. Grieve what's broken. Accept that suffering is only temporary. God will transform your brokenness into something beautiful and new.

REFLECT ON YOUR STORY

1. *How is God inviting you to deepen your faith—what is the cup before you?*

2. *Beauty is healing. Explore ways that you can make space for more beauty in your life. How can you bring more beauty into your everyday life?*

3. *What One Word speaks to you today?*

PRAY & REST

A SIMPLE PRACTICE: PRAYER OF SURRENDER

C.S. Lewis said, "For most of us the prayer in Gethsemane is the only model. Removing mountains can wait." American Trappist monk Thomas Merton in *The Seven Storey Mountain* agrees: "The more you try to avoid suffering, the more you suffer." Are you or someone you love discouraged or suffering?

What is Jesus saying to you in this place? How does the One Word Prayer *BROKENNESS* speak to you? Offer a Prayer of Surrender.

Jesus, this is what I'm afraid of happening. I don't want this . . .

Jesus, what I hear you saying to me . . .

Jesus, not my will but yours. I surrender these things . . .

TODAY'S BELOVED CHALLENGE

Listen to Classical Music

*Classical music is proven to relieve stress,
improve your mood, and boost creativity.*

Feed your soul with beautiful music. Let God begin to heal you.

Listening to Classical Music Heals the Soul

SOUL CARE TRAIL NOTES

It's amazing how our God designed our bodies to heal. Listening to beautiful classical music heals our souls too. Innumerable studies show the incredible mental and physical benefits of listening to classical music. Scientists found that simply playing classical music as background ambience significantly improves your mood and productivity.

Here are seven benefits of listening to classical music:

1. Makes you happy: Releases dopamine, activating the brain's pleasure center.
2. Reduces stress and anxiety: Tempos resemble a restful human heartbeat.
3. Fights depression: Eases and lifts depressive symptoms.
4. Relieves pain: Patients used significantly less pain medication.
5. Improves sleep: Listening for forty-five minutes prior to bed improves sleep quality.
6. Boosts creativity, memory, and energizes: Infuses tasks with enjoyment.
7. Lowers blood pressure.

∂ ∂ ∂

New

You are beautiful to me. I am making all things new.

You don't have to wait until you're completely new
To be you.

You don't have to wait until you are free of doubt
To step into the light. To be seen.

You don't have to try so hard
To understand everything.

What no one sees, God whispers—
You are beautiful to me.

"Behold, I am making all things new...in you."

INSPIRED BY REVELATION 21:5

"Our hearts are restless, until they can find rest in you."

SAINT AUGUSTINE

As love heals our hearts, Jesus calls us to a new way of living. A new way of *being*.

He invites us to make changes that match with our new identity—as the Beloved. He invites us to walk by faith. When we hold on to Jesus' hands, uncertainty isn't something to be avoided, but a sure sign that faith is pointing us in the right direction—toward what our hearts really long for. God's creative work of renewal is *you*.

If we only walked the road we understood and could guarantee, we would never go where Jesus wants to take us. We would never be changed. We would walk by sight instead.

As you prepare to step out into new beginnings, to dare to *live the life of the Beloved in reality*, you may find what I've experienced: I can go from inspired to discouraged easily.

Jesus always shows me just one next step. But I become discouraged if I stop and try to figure out how things are going to end up—where one step will lead. That's when a simple idea suddenly becomes overwrought with worry, and then those worries choke the joy out of the idea. And I end up doing nothing at all.

When we actually step out to be who God created us to be, we become vulnerable to the critical voices that once kept us safe from hurt or uncertainty—but left us unchanged.

But we are learning to follow Jesus with our hearts. And because this is a new journey, *it's okay to be insecure and doubtful*, because it means that we're living in a new way.

A New Way

This new way of living as the Beloved may feel disorienting and even cause us to feel anxious:

I don't understand how.
I can't do this.
This is too hard.

When we pray these private words, sometimes only silence echoes back. So much is happening outside of our control. Panic can set in.

Panic happens when you fear life will change for the worse. But despair happens *when you fear nothing will ever change.* When you feel that *you* will never change.

That's the moment we can easily retreat to our old ways of staying safe and not trying anything new. Let's not retreat anymore, friends.

As I pictured myself walking on the same long, dusty road I've walked all these years—giving up on myself again—I whispered to Jesus, *I've come so far. I don't want to give up. But I don't know what to do.*

Jesus won't leave us in the middle of our journeys. Jesus invites us to enter into a scene from the Easter story.

The Journey Back

Two friends were walking with their backs bent, their hearts broken, and their hopes for tomorrow dashed to pieces. Their hope had died on a cross. And now, they were walking back to where they'd journeyed so far.

They were returning to life as they knew it. They had lost all hope that life could be different. That *they* could change.

The two friends were walking in the opposite direction of where they'd once found hope. So much so, they did not recognize who was walking with them. They spent the entire journey back, returning to Emmaus, talking about how everything was ruined, wrong, and lost back in Jerusalem.

Meanwhile a quiet stranger they met on the road patiently listened to the whole story, from start to finish, told in exhausting detail. He didn't interrupt. He didn't judge. He didn't say, "What's wrong with you? It's me! Can't you see?"

No. Instead, this stranger named Jesus asked them questions. He wanted to hear more. *Oh? What happened? Tell me more . . .*

Jesus was curious. He wanted to hear all about their despair.

READ GOD'S STORY

Jesus tells us through this scene from the Easter story:

> *That silence you hear as you pour out your heart?*
> *It's me. I'm listening. To you.*
> *Walking with you.*
> *Even as your heart's running*
> *in the opposite direction of hope,*
> *I am with you.*

When we are clouded by our doubts, it's hard to recognize Jesus' presence. It's okay, because Jesus is walking with us the same way He walked with the two friends.

> "They urged him, saying,
> 'Stay with us,
> for it is getting toward evening,
> and the day is now nearly over.'
> So he went in to stay with them.

When he had reclined at the table with them,
He took the bread and breaking it,
He began giving it to them.

Then their eyes were opened
and they recognized him…

They said to one another,
'Were not our hearts burning within us
while he was speaking to us on the road?'"

LUKE 24:29–32

Jesus broke bread with them—right in the midst of their place of retreat. By the time they had finished confiding in him, they recognized that the quiet stranger who walked beside them was actually their friend. Jesus. Jesus is showing us that he is with us on the road.

✑ *God's Whispers to You*

Beloved,
You can be new. We've come so far together.
Tell me all your doubts and questions.
I want to hear all about them. Tell me more.

I won't give up on you.
I am making all things new—in you.
I love you.

Hearts burning. It's what you feel when God's whispers touch your heart. Our pounding heartbeats are resting against

His strong and loving embrace. I'm stepping out to be me. And so you can you.

Putting off the old, putting on the new. You and I can do both. We can be happy, joy filled, celebrating the resurrection of the *new me* Jesus is bringing back to life. In the same moment, we can also carry sorrow, imperfection, and insecurity—even despair—*because both the old and the new are found in his embrace.* Because in this journey of faith, both the old and the new are moving into the light.

It's the Living Way. This faith of real flesh and bone. Spirit and soul. Jesus in you and me.

☞ *A Prayer for Today*: *God, Make All Things New!*

"Behold, I am making all things new…in you."
INSPIRED BY REVELATION 21:5

Dear Jesus,
I don't want to wait until I'm perfect
to spread my wings.
I don't want to wait until there is no more sorrow,
to celebrate the moments of joy you want to give to me.

Give me courage
to step out in a new way—
to say yes to whatever you have for me today.
and say no to the old ways.
Thank you for making all things new in me.
Amen.

Jesus loves you completely. Unconditionally. Irrevocably. Again and again.

Let Easter come alive in you today. Let's get up and do what our two friends from Emmaus did. They headed back to Jerusalem. With hope.

They returned to tell everyone what had happened on their journey. How Jesus walked with them. How they recognized him.

This time, they were changed. They were new.

It's time for us to do the same. Let's walk as new people. *Beloved.* Today.

Give Yourself Permission: Experience something new. Feed your soul with the five senses: sight, sound, smell, touch, taste. Invest time or money. Be patient. Let go of goals when trying new things. You are *becoming,* not achieving.

REFLECT ON YOUR STORY

1. *How is Jesus calling you to step out and be new?*

2. *What do you see God making new in your life?*

3. *What One Word speaks to your heart today?*

PRAY & REST

A SIMPLE PRACTICE: LIFE VERSE MEDITATION

When the Psalmist couldn't pray, he turned to meditation. "I was too troubled to speak...I will *remember*...I will *meditate* on all your works" (Psalm 77:4, 11–12).

Old Testament scholar Bruce Waltke explains: "Meditation is a chance for me to stop talking and listen to God. I don't hear an audible voice, but I find the Lord...fill[s] my mind with His thoughts. *This isn't a form of inspiration, but illumination.* Write your thoughts down. Sometimes my heart burns within me."

Today's One Word Prayer is *NEW.* What special "Life Verse" encourages you? Meditate on it for five minutes. Let God illuminate you with something new.

Jesus, I remember what you once said to me in (write your special life verse):

🌿 🌿 🌿

TODAY'S BELOVED CHALLENGE

Make Plans for a Fun Weekend
Try something new. Or enjoy a favorite pleasure.

Read a good book, enjoy dinner with a friend or a date night, see a movie, play minigolf with the kids, knit, or bake some muffins. Jesus is making all things new.

SOUL CARE TRAIL NOTES

Plan Your Weekend and Experience More Joy

The two friends from Emmaus were changed after enjoying a meal with Jesus. When a big issue looms over you, plan something enjoyable for the weekend, knowing Jesus is with you. Simply making plans revitalizes you with what psychologists call *anticipatory joy*.

Research at the University of London showed that when people made plans to enjoy something later—it didn't have to be large or significant—they experienced high levels of well-being by anticipating the experience *before* anything happened. One study found that people merely thinking about watching their favorite movies raised their endorphin levels by 27 percent. Another showed that planning a vacation brought peak happiness during the weeks leading up to the actual vacation. So don't want until your troubles are over. Make plans to refill your soul with joy or peace as is. Today.

PART FIVE

Daring as the Beloved

———————— 🌿 🌿 🌿 ————————

Live Courageously: Be Known

As you heal your yesterday,
God will call you to radically step into your
belovedness *today*.
To love *and* be loved.

Jesus whispers,
Dare to be known.
Dare to blossom.

The following devotionals dare you
to make bold changes in your self-talk,
your friendships, and your schedule.

Each day inspires you to live courageously
and put God's love into action
in your heart and with others.

"I will give you a new heart and put a new spirit in you;
I will remove from you your heart of stone and give you a
heart of flesh."
EZEKIEL 36:26

Play

Let me love you first. Dare to be renewed.

God,
help me make room
for the most intimate part
of my soul to come alive again.

I hear you whispering—
Let me love you first.

Renew your joy in me once again.

*"But those who hope in the Lord will renew their
strength… They will run and not grow weary, they will
walk and not be faint."* ISAIAH 40:31

"The nature of this flower is to bloom." ALICE WALKER

I had never picked peaches before.

Maybe that doesn't seem like such a big deal. But for someone born in California, living near the fruit capital of the world, it's kind of embarrassing.

One day when my friend Sally, who had retired to Brentwood (a town known for fruit orchards), mentioned that her daughter and grandkids were visiting to pick peaches, my favorite summer fruit, *I decided to take a dare.*

"Maybe Eric, the boys, and I can visit you and Mike sometime. Maybe we can go peach picking together?" I tried to act casual. Half serious, half joking.

"We'd love to. What day's good for you?" Sally replied. A date was set.

Out in the orchard, I felt like a little girl again, having fun with the boys, climbing ladders and picking peaches big as snow globes off the trees.

But I was surprised by what happened after we got back to the house. Sally said we were making fresh peach cobblers. She took out a stockpot and started boiling water.

Why was she boiling water? What happened next was even more bizarre. Sally started throwing our beloved peaches into the pot.

"Aren't we baking? Why are you boiling the peaches?" I asked. My boys, Josh and Caleb, scrambled over to see.

Sally smiled. "Let me show you." She rolled the floating peaches out with a ladle. Then, placed them in the sink, under cool running water.

The peaches steamed as she took a paring knife and began to lift the skin back from its golden flesh. *Sally was peeling peaches.*

As I stood there watching Sally, my boys crowded in, eyes wide as saucers. The water glistened over the peaches turning in her hand, catching the sunlight glimmering through the kitchen windows—and I felt God whisper ever so gently,

I love you, Bonnie.
I love you, Josh and Caleb.
I love you.

Over and again, God's whispers of love wouldn't stop echoing, as tears of joy flowed. You see, I've never had a grandmother show me how to make peach cobblers. Neither did my kids.

But God knew. God sees deep into our souls, and He uses simple everyday joys to whisper words of love to you and me.

Dare to Play and Be Renewed

In one simple moment, God lavished love on us with joy and peace through my friends, who were enjoying something so everyday ordinary to them, they were totally unaware that anything special was happening.

What is the joy God's longing to rewrite into your life? Will you lay down your heart and your schedule to let God renew you with joy?

Dare to play. Make the time. Allow yourself to be interrupted by God. Dare to take the risk to ask, to go, or to try. *Take steps to receive.*

Play is important, because when you give yourself permission to feel joy again, you experience God's presence. *You become the Beloved.* Reclaim the simple moments of joy. Hear God whisper: *Joy was meant for you.*

Look Deeper

What are the everyday things that once made you happy—that renewed your spirit? Maybe there is something seemingly ordinary you enjoyed during a simpler time in your life, and you thought it wasn't anything special. But as you look back now, *you realize it made your soul come alive.* It gave you joy.

See Jesus loving you in those moments of joy. Hear him whispering, *I love you*—over and over. God takes the most ordinary things others may not find noteworthy, and He *uses those very things to love us and love others through us.*

It's like turning water into wine. Jesus longs to turn water into wine—through *you.*

▓▓▓▓▓ READ GOD'S STORY ▓▓▓▓▓

Listen now as Jesus takes us to another kitchen among pots of water, too. It's a wedding banquet where the wine ran out and joy was at risk—*where everyone was unaware that anything special was happening.*

> *"Standing nearby were six stone water jars. Jesus said to the servants,*
> *"Fill the jars with water"; so they filled them to the brim.*
>
> *'Now draw some out and take it to the master of the banquet.'*
>
> *They did so, and the master of the banquet tasted the water that had been turned into wine.*
>
> *He did not realize where it had come from and said,*
> *'Everyone brings out the choice wine first*

*and then the cheaper wine after the guests have had
too much to drink; but you have saved the best until
now.'"*

JOHN 2:6–10

It's never too late for joy. God saves the best for last. You are that jar God wants to fill with joy today, turning water into wine through His love for you.

Like me, you may be good of taking care of everybody else, prioritizing the urgent and getting things done well, but you've placed your own joy and well-being last.

See Jesus now quietly, lovingly taking your hands into his to whisper—*Let me love you first.*

"We love each other because God loved us first."

1 JOHN 4:19

✑ *God's Whispers to You*

Dear Beloved,
Your peace and joy is important to me.
Dare to let me in. Draw closer.

Dare to lay your weary heart next to me.
Let me turn water into wine—in you.
Let me love you first.

Renew your joy with me once again.

Like a flickering flame never to be extinguished, the Holy Spirit uses simple joys to renew you with God's love. Then watch him use it to love others through you.

✍ A Prayer for Today: Give Me Courage to Be Renewed

"But those who hope in the Lord will renew their strength… They will run and not grow weary, they will walk and not be faint."   ISAIAH 40:31

Dear Jesus,
Give me courage to reclaim moments of joy today.
To take time for myself.
To play and be renewed.

Renew my mind to see a vision for who I am
when I'm revitalized with joy—with you.

Then inspire a new idea
to invite a friend to enjoy something simple
together with you—through me.
Thank you.
Amen.

The gift of time. The gift of presence. The gift of joy. These are the things that really matter. They feed the soul.

Take time to enjoy what brings you joy today. Then you will be able to offer that joy to others—your children, your husband, your friends, and even strangers. Because the truth is, we all get a little weary on the journey of life.

We can refresh each other with joy. Together, the journey will be lighter, kinder, and more beautiful. You may be unaware you could offer anything special in your joy. But you don't need to know how it will happen. Jesus will turn water into wine in you and through you.

But you must first step out. *Dare to be renewed*. Dare to play. Today.

Give Yourself Permission: Make time to play. Be child-like. Laugh, waste some time, sing, dance, try something new. Renew your spirit with joy.

REFLECT ON YOUR STORY

1. *What can you do today to renew your spirit with joy? How can you play?*

2. *What One Word speaks to you in today's Scriptures?*

PRAY & REST

A SIMPLE PRACTICE: ABBA PRAYER

Today, offer an Abba Prayer. Simply talk to God as an affectionate father. Use a two-phrase prayer—*Abba Father* (breathe in), *I'm yours* (breathe out)—or share unfiltered. Share anything inspired by today's One Word Prayer, *PLAY.*

New Testament scholar N.T. Wright writes, "The Lord's Prayer is not so much a command as an invitation . . . to share in the prayer-life of Jesus himself." We talk to God as our father *freely* like Jesus did. "For you did not receive a spirit of slavery to fall back into fear, but . . . with this Spirit, we cry, 'Abba, Father' " (Romans 8:15).

Dear Abba Father . . . (let your prayer flow freely)

꧁ ꧁ ꧁

TODAY'S BELOVED CHALLENGE

Dare to Play
Do Something That Makes You Smile
Take time for joy.

Joy is important to God and to your health. Be His child. Play.

Prioritize Play and Revitalize Your Joy

Play isn't just for kids. Tap into the powerful benefits of play, shown by neurophysiology research: improved mood and well-being, reducing anxiety, depression, stimulating creativity, and enhancing relationships.

That's what psychiatrist Stuart Brown calls the "state of play" in his book *Play*, studying the role of play in everyone—from criminals and business people to artists and Nobel Prize winners. Play is "purposeless, fun and pleasurable. Play is the purest expression of love." There is no goal, but joy.

Add play into your life. "Go backward to the most joyful experience. How does that connect to your life now? Enrich your life by prioritizing play." Brown outlines *eight play personalities* in his book:

The Joker—nonsensical play, fun, silly
The Kinesthete—body play, physical movement
The Explorer—experiential play, exploring physically (places), intellectually (new ideas), relationally (meeting people), emotionally (music, art, story)
The Competitor—group play, engaged in team games or one-on-one

The Director—organizing play, orchestrating events, people, parties, projects, movies, music, plays
The Collector—objects or experiences
The Artists/Creator—creative play, making things
The Storyteller—imaginative play, experiencing and expressing a story or character's actions, thoughts, and emotions

What's your play personality? Explore and discover.

֍ ֍ ֍

Known

Dare to be refreshed. Dare to be known.

We are all in the middle of something.
What gives us strength for the journey
is to know we are not alone.

We need friends to share the journey.

*"Your love has given me much joy and comfort,
because you, brother, have refreshed the hearts of the
Lord's people."*   PHILEMON 1:7

Oh, the comfort—the inexpressible comfort of feeling safe with a person—having either to weigh thoughts nor measure words, but pouring them all right out, just as they are, chaff and grain together; certain that a faithful hand will take and sift them, keep what is worth keeping, and then with the breath of kindness blow the rest away.   DINAH CRAIK

Dim sum.

That's what the Chinese call their teatime. It translates as *touching the heart*. It begins with a cup of tea. Before you sit down, the waiter asks what kind you'd like. By the time you've asked your friend *how are you*, a pot of hot tea arrives at your table.

For a moment in time, you and your friend can put the world on pause. You wait for bite-sized, tapas-like dishes to make their way to you. Your chopsticks clink on a small plate, dabbed with soy sauce and chili paste swirled together, like a painter's palette. Instead of a paintbrush, you dip shrimp dumplings wrapped in translucent rice flour, steamed fresh from the kitchen, where half a dozen hands artfully make each one you place in your mouth.

Dim sum is linked to the centuries old tradition of drinking tea—*yum chai*—which began with *travelers needing a place to rest* on the ancient Silk Road in China. As merchants traveled long journeys to sell their goods, teahouses dotting the roadside gave sojourners respite and refreshment.

Because we are all on the journey of faith, we need a place to rest and refresh. We are all in the middle of something. *We need time to refresh our souls with friendship. We need the refuge of a friend in the middle of our journeys.*

What truly revitalizes our souls is what we often hide: our

unfinished stories. Because, you see, we all face unknown chapters, vulnerable to questions we can't answer and unexpected turns when life goes off script.

What gives us strength for the journey is to know we are not alone.

Dare to Be Refreshed. Dare to Be Known.

Do you long to be refreshed? To step out as the Beloved, stop and refresh your soul with a friend. *Dare to be known.* Share your unfinished stories.

Like me, you may be good at connecting with people to get things done. It's easier to keep busy and build friendships based on what you think others want and need from you. But *we weren't created to journey alone. We need friends to welcome us as we live our stories, unfiltered.*

But what often keeps us isolated is wounds from hurtful friendships. Even with all our online 24/7 technology, studies show we are the loneliest generation. *We've lost the intimacy of being known.* We've become adept at connecting with lots of people on social media about things we do and how to do them. But we hide who we are and how we feel. We are all desperately lonely.

Jesus understands our loneliness. When he sent his disciples two by two on their first mission, he told them to "shake the dust off your feet." He knew rejection would be part of the journey. Yet Jesus still calls us to find refreshment among friends, "Take nothing for the journey. Carry no purse, no bread, no bag, no money" (Luke 9:3).

In other words, Jesus is telling us—*Don't give up. Keep being vulnerable. You will find a friend who will provide what you need for the journey.*

Dare to be refreshed by friends. Stop and allow others to know you.

READ GOD'S STORY

Maybe like me, there was no one you could trust with your heart and your needs. But staying silent with our stories comes at a cost. *There is no greater burden than an untold story.* God whispers:

"Carry one another's burdens." GALATIANS 6:2

*"Two are better than one…
For if either of them falls, the one will lift up his companion.*

Furthermore, if two lie down together they keep warm, but how can one be warm alone?

And if one can overpower him who is alone, two can resist him." ECCLESIASTES 4:9–12

This passage is often read at weddings, but these words were meant for everyday travelers who had to walk from town to town. They were exposed to the cold elements and robbers at night, when they stopped to sleep and rest. We all need this comfort and security: a friend to refresh us on the journey.

Are you also in the middle of an unfinished story on your journey of faith? *Is God inviting you to find a friend to carry the burden with you?* Then, take the risk. Invite someone in. Dare to be known.

✏ *God's Whispers to You*

*Beloved,
I see your ache for friendship. How you've been hurt.
Don't give up.*

I am with you. I will help you.
Like tea leaves, softening as they steep,
you carry a fragrance,
released each moment you stop to rest
with another pilgrim of faith.

Together, we'll find a friend to share the journey.
Be brave. Refresh your heart.
Share your story, so a friend can share hers in return.

This world is very busy, friends. Constantly marketing and branding ourselves, we've forgotten what makes us real: love. But you and I are beloved. We are invited to live radically different. *Counterculture.*

Time is a holy gift we can give each other in this world preoccupied by influence. When we stop and rest together, we say to each other, *You are loved. You are worth it. You are friend. As you are.*

Can you imagine what beautiful and holy gift it would be to invite a friend for coffee, to ride a bike, walk a trail, bake cookies, or go out for dinner?

✆ *A Prayer for Today:* *Give Me Courage to Be Known*

"Your love has given me much joy and comfort,
because you, brother, have refreshed the hearts of the
Lord's people." PHILEMON 1:7

Dear Jesus,
Give me grace to move forward
from the rejection you so fully understand.

Guide me to find new friends
and rekindle old ones.
To stop and welcome each other,
to rest and refresh.

Give me courage to be countercultural,
to make time for friendship
to share our stories
and dare to be known.
Amen.

Dim sum. Touch the heart. *Friendship.* It's food for the soul. Dare to share your unfinished story. Dare to be known. Be refreshed.

Give Yourself Permission: Make time for friendship. Refresh your heart with real soul-to-soul conversations. Be vulnerable. Prioritize one-on-one time with a friend or two. Stop off the road of busyness.

REFLECT ON YOUR STORY

1. *How can you refresh your heart with friendship?*

2. *How can you be countercultural and carve space and time for friendship?*

3. *What One Word speaks to you today?*

PRAY & REST

A SIMPLE PRACTICE: PRAYERS FOR FRIENDSHIP

Christian counselor and author Larry Crabb writes, "When spiritual friends share their stories...They rest. There's nothing to fix, nothing to improve...Gather with other travelers on the narrow road, pilgrims who acknowledge their confusion and feel their fears. Then, together, live those questions in [God's] Presence."

Today, pray for friendship. We need friends to encourage us and share joy. Jesus calls *us* friends. Using today's One Word Prayer, *KNOWN*, choose one of the eight prayer prompts below to inspire you to pray about friendships in your life:

Longing	*Forgiveness*	*Changing*	*Spouse*
Thankful	*Healing*	*Good-bye*	*Children*

Jesus, this is my One Word Prayer for friendship. Refresh, bless, and help me...

TODAY'S BELOVED CHALLENGE

Invite a Friend for Girls' Night Out
Schedule dinner, breakfast, or coffee.
Take time for in-real-life friendship.

Be countercultural. Make time for friends. It matters to God.

SOUL CARE TRAIL NOTES

Wholehearted Friendship Destresses and Lengthens Life

In our digital age, it's easy to mistakenly substitute online connections with in-real-life friendships. Research shows using social sites doesn't translate to closer offline relationships. It is real, quality friendships that reduce stress, boost happiness, lengthen life, and build a stronger immune system. Studies tell us that having friends to tell our stories to—wholehearted, honest sharing, uncrafted emotions, and moments about the events happening—builds emotional resilience. Storytelling helps us bounce back months after we confide in someone.

So stop off the road of busyness. Revitalize your soul with a friend. Share your stories.

❧ ❧ ❧

Change

Renovate your heart. Dare to change.

The only certainty I'm beginning to understand
I'll ever have in this life is God's unchanging love.

My one certainty is you, Jesus.
Renovate my heart.
Help me dare to change.

"I will give you a new heart and put a new spirit in you;
I will remove from you your heart of stone and give you a
heart of flesh."   EZEKIEL 36:26

"A story only matters, I suspect, to the extent that the people in the story change." NEIL GAIMAN

Chinatown was last on my list.

It's where I was born, but its streets are loaded with memories I didn't want to revisit. But Anne Marie, wife of a U.S. military chaplain, was visiting San Francisco from Nashville and she had one request: "I have always been intimidated by Chinatown," she wrote. "If you're can serve as guide, I'd love to go."

I mapped our way to my favorite Chinese bakery and went into autopilot "tour guide" mode, pointing out everything, when suddenly Anne Marie stopped at a storefront.

She peeked into a room with walls lined with rows of glass canisters labeled with Chinese characters and their English translations—for tea leaves. It was a tea-tasting room. As I followed her in, the woman behind the counter pointed us to sit down. *Would we like a tea-tasting session?*

Yes! Anne Marie answered. So I sat down.

Our hostess asked what tea we wanted to taste. I found myself answering, "Bo Lei." *Bo Lei* is a fermented black tea from China's Yunnan province. It's the first tea I drank as a little girl, sitting with my mother at meals, watching tea leaves swirl in my cup as I sipped.

Our server pinched some leaves into my teacup, poured near-boiling water in, and swished the leaves a few shakes. Then to my shock, she turned the cup upside down, throwing out my tea.

I had forgotten. In the Chinese brewing style, before steeping it to drink, the first brewing of tea is the cleansing rinse. *She was washing the tea leaves to awaken the tea.*

Washing the tea with hot water softens and opens the leaves to release aroma—imbuing it with personality, body, rich tones and flavor. Dust gathers as tea is dried on the floor, so washing the tea leaves gives it a clean and smooth texture, lifting away the bitterness and yielding sweetness.

It's the second brew that is worth savoring.

Dare to be Changed

Over the years, you may have collected some memories that have tasted bitter or have left your soul dry. But underneath it all, there is a part of you still young like a child, smoky with sweetness, waiting to be reawakened. God longs to revitalize that part of you by calling you to change.

To say new things. Do things differently.
Make radical choices or quietly begin something small.
To grieve what's been lost or recover and rejoice when it's found.

Jesus may be inviting you to turn over your heart to him— for a second brew.

Let go of your plans and break out of autopilot mode. **Dare to be changed.**

READ GOD'S STORY

Allow the Holy Spirit to wash you anew with God's whispers of rest. See Jesus cleansing you with love, bringing change. Changing *you*. Hear Jesus calling you to renovate your life as the Beloved:

"No one pours new wine into old wineskins.
If he does, the wine will burst the skins,

and both the wine and the wineskins will be ruined.
Instead, new wine is poured into new wineskins."

MARK 2:22

Give yourself permission to make changes that align with your new identity as the Beloved. Dare to be his.

✐ *God's Whispers to You*

Dear Beloved,
Whenever you wonder if anything can change,
remember everything beautiful
will be made new once more in you—with me.

I will help you. I will restore you.
Let me renovate your heart.
It's time for change so you can hold new wine in new
wineskins.
Release the fragrance of my love breathing—alive—in you.

Like anything crafted with quality, renovation takes time. Follow God's voice and allow yourself to be guided and changed. Like the fragrance of tea, the beauty of whom God made you will blossom.

"But thank God, who is always leading us through
Christ… He releases the fragrance of the knowledge
of him everywhere through us.
For we are the fragrance of Christ."

2 CORINTHIANS 2:14–15

✎ A Prayer for Today:
Give Me Courage to Change

*"I will give you a new heart and put a new spirit in you;
I will remove from you your heart of stone and give you a
heart of flesh."*   EZEKIEL 36:26

Dear Jesus,
Renovate my heart.
Renew in me a willing spirit.

Give me courage to be changed.
Help me to be bold to make the changes
you're inviting me to make today.
With you.
Amen.

As the sweet fragrance of my childhood tea returned to
me that morning in Chinatown, happiness filled my soul.
My friend Anne Marie looked over with teacup in hand. "It's
good, isn't it?" she said, smiling.

"Yes. It's really good." I laughed, my tears making me a
little more whole.

Step out as the Beloved. *Dare to be changed.* Be the real you.
Today.

Give Yourself Permission: Make time to renovate your
heart. Get out of your comfort zone. Be inconvenienced.
Change your lifestyle, your schedule, your mind, your
story, or your plans. Do things radically different or quietly small.

REFLECT ON YOUR STORY

1. *What change is God prompting you to make to renovate your heart and life?*

2. *What One Word speaks to you today's Scriptures?*

PRAY & REST

A SIMPLE PRACTICE: OPEN DOOR PRAYER

Today, let's pray for an *Open Door to change our hearts*. "Pray for us, that God may open a door for our message, so that we may [speak] the mystery of Christ, for which I am in chains" (Colossians 4:3). It's amazing that the apostle Paul didn't ask to change his imprisonment, but to *be the change agent himself.* As is.

Writer and theologian Frederick Buechner inspires our prayer prompt: "Listen to your life. Listen to what happens to you because it is through what happens to you that God speaks... It was not so much that a door opened as that I suddenly found a door open all along which I only just then stumbled upon."

What's happening in your life? What is God saying to you? Listen quietly. Pray.

Jesus, I see you opening these doors of CHANGE in my life—inviting me to...

TODAY'S BELOVED CHALLENGE

Brew a Cup of Tea

*Savor the soothing benefits of
chamomile, peppermint, or your favorite tea.
Replenish your mind and body.*

Each day brings change. Give yourself space to breathe.
Enjoy teatime with Jesus. "So whether you eat or drink…
do it all for the glory of God" (1 Corinthians 10:31).

SOUL CARE
TRAIL
NOTES

Calm Anxiety by Drinking Tea

With change comes inherent stress. Calm anxiety by drinking tea and enjoying the therapeutic benefits. Here are three favorites, but there are many others!

- *Chamomile tea* helps eliminate insomnia and mood issues, like depression. Research supports chamomile's ability to smooth muscle fibers and relax blood vessels, contributing to sleep. Even the fragrance of chamomile lowers a stress hormone in the brain, reducing anxiety, easing headaches and tummyaches.
- *Peppermint tea* has a calming effect that combats stress, and the menthol acts as a muscle relaxant, easing headaches, digestion, and abdominal pain.
- *Black tea* contains an amino acid that reduces the effects of a stressful event. One study showed a 20 percent drop in cortisol after drinking black tea.

Listen

Reinvigorate your spirit. Dare to listen.

God,
give me the courage to choose
the quiet, unknown journey
you're inviting me to experience with you,
instead of pursuing a step-by-step plan
I'm driven to accomplish for you.

Let me dare to be still.
Speak, Lord. I'm listening.

*"I call on you, my God, for you will answer me;
turn your ear to me and hear my prayer."*   PSALM 17:6

❧ ❧ ❧

"'You would not have called to me unless I had been calling to you,' said the Lion."

C. S. LEWIS, *THE SILVER CHAIR*

The question popped out of the blue, as I tucked ten-year-old Josh into bed. Somehow, the most creative conversations emerge at lights out.

"How do you hear God talk to you?" Josh began rapid-firing more questions, as I scrambled to find a simple answer. "What does His voice actually sound like? How do you know whether it's your imagination or God?" I detected a slight grin, as I turned the lights back on.

I gave the standard answers: how God talks to us as we read the Bible, how the Holy Spirit speaks as we pray and through other believers as they share and teach. I reminded Josh of all the prayers God had answered for him.

"I know. But you talk about hearing God's whispers. The Bible talks about Abraham and David hearing from God. I'm worried. I know God loves me, but..." Josh hesitated to say what came next. "Mom, I've never heard God actually talk to me. Does that make me bad? Why can't I hear Him?"

As my son's eyes filled with concern, I knew he wasn't a little boy anymore, satisfied with Sunday school answers. My son was on a journey of faith and he needed what we all need: *reassurance that God's voice was his to experience.*

"No, you are not bad at all," I assured Josh. "It's the opposite. You're growing up, son. Your friendship with God is *going deeper.*

"You don't want to just know *about* Him. *You want to hear Him speak to your heart—just to you.* In a personal way.

"The fact that you're wanting to hear His voice is evidence.

The Holy Spirit is in you. That desire is God touching your heart. He's speaking to you!"

"Really?" Josh perked up with curiosity. I told him I had the same questions when I was a little. *I told him I'm still learning to hear God's voice in new ways—because that's how a friendship grows.*

"It's a good and beautiful thing," I whispered to Josh. "It means your faith is real, son. It's alive—growing."

I asked Josh to listen to a story—of another boy who found it hard to hear God, even though God was talking to him. It's a story we're invited to listen to today as well.

Something Different

One night, while lying in bed, trying to sleep, God spoke to this little boy for the first time—*Samuel! Samuel!*

God was whispering his name. But because hearing God was a new experience, *he didn't recognize God's voice.*

Are you longing to hear God's voice—fresh and in a new way? Is busyness keeping you from recognizing God's Voice of Love in everyday life?

Samuel, who was living in the temple, ran over to Eli the priest, thinking Eli was calling him. It happened three times. In the same way, *we can easily run from one thing to another*, answering other voices that demand doing, work, fear, and busyness.

But the fourth time God called him, *Samuel did something different.* Samuel dared to listen.

READ GOD'S STORY

Listen now as God invites us to do the same:

> *"A third time the Lord called, 'Samuel!'*
> *And Samuel got up and went to Eli and said, 'Here I am;*
> *you called me.'*

Then Eli realized that the Lord was calling the boy.
So Eli told Samuel, "Go and lie down, and if he calls you,
say,

'Speak, Lord, for your servant is listening.'"
So Samuel went and lay down in his place.
The Lord came and stood there, calling as at the other
times,
'Samuel! Samuel!'

Then Samuel said, 'Speak, for your servant is listening.'
And the Lord said to Samuel: 'See, I am about to do
something…'"   1 SAMUEL 3:8–11

In other words, Samuel whispered, "*Speak, Lord. I'm here.*
I'm listening."

Something beautiful and new sparked his soul the moment
Samuel dared to listen. He gave God time and space to speak: *His*
living word.

Today, God is waiting for your invitation. He longs to revitalize your soul the same way. With His voice. Dare to nourish
your heart. Dare to spend one-on-one time with God. *Dare to*
be still and listen.

I'm here. I'm listening. This is the prayer I invited Josh to
whisper that night. It's the prayer God longs to hear from you
and me. So He can draw near.

"God may not answer right away tonight," I told Josh. "But
He will. In a personal, quiet way. *Just to you.* God knows your
love language. God will speak."

"What if I still can't hear Him?" Josh asked.

"Then God will keep speaking until you do. Remember?
God didn't stop calling Samuel until he heard Him." I said this
to encourage myself as much as Josh. Because the truth was, I

wanted God to speak right then and there to Josh. "I wonder what He'll say, huh?" I smiled to reassure him. "I'll pray for you until it happens," I promised.

As you can imagine, I prayed that night to ask God, *Please speak to my son, Jesus.* God reassured me with His whispers of rest.

✐ *God's Whispers to You*

Beloved,
I'm here. I'm listening. To you.

Every unspoken word,
I hear your every whisper.
Every question.
Every desire for my voice—
echoes my heartbeat in you.

Say the word.
And I'll whisper words of love.
Just for you.

Give God space to touch your heart. Take time to enjoy God in quietness. Journal. Light a candle. Talk a walk. Take a bath.

Make space to slow down—to still yourself and rest. Spend time with God. Just you and Him alone. In nature. With music. Color, paint, craft.

Enjoy something that brings your spirit peace or joy. Notice what's beautiful around you. Find God's love notes. *Give Him a chance to whisper to you.*

No Longer Servants

Today, on the resurrected side of the cross, Jesus no longer calls us servants. Jesus calls us friends. He calls us Beloved.

> *"No longer do I call you servants…But I have called you friends, for everything that I have heard from my Father I have made known to you."* JOHN 15:15

This is why now we can pray: *Speak, for your Beloved is listening.*

✐ *A Prayer for Today:*
Give Me Courage to Be Still and Listen

> *"I call on you, my God, for you will answer me;*
> *turn your ear to me and hear my prayer."* PSALM 17:6

Dear Jesus,
Speak, Lord, your Beloved is listening.

I miss you.
I want to spend time with you today.

Reinvigorate my soul.
Open the eyes of my heart.
Say the word. And I'll be in your arms again.

Give me the courage to choose
the quiet, unknown journey
you're inviting me to experience with you,

instead of pursuing a step-by-step plan
I'm driven to accomplish for you.

Let me dare to be still.
Fill me with your Holy Spirit.
Speak, Lord, I'm listening.
Amen.

Just as God actually stood next to Samuel in the temple, whispering his name, your heart is God's temple. Jesus is right here with you, whispering your name.

Ask God to speak. Then do what Samuel did. Rest. Wait. Keep listening.

A few weeks went by after Josh prayed to hear God speak. Then, after church one Sunday, on the car ride back home, Josh told us, "Mom, Dad—I felt God speak to me! The song we were singing in worship spoke to me because I felt they were *my* words. I felt the Holy Spirit flooding my heart. I felt a connection to God. It made me feel happy and joyful!" And we all cheered.

No matter where you are or what you're doing, *be invigorated. Dare to listen.*

Hear God lovingly whisper to you—*I'm here. With you. I'm listening.*

Give Yourself Permission: Make time to be still and listen. Reinvigorate your spirit *with God's voice.* Explore your love language with God. Carve out *Me Time* to go where you don't have to do anything for anyone, except to be alone to rest, refresh and feel close to God again.

REFLECT ON YOUR STORY

1. *Do you miss spending time with Jesus? What places bring you rest, to hear God or feel close to Him best?*

2. *What One Word speaks to you today?*

PRAY & REST

A SIMPLE PRACTICE: LISTENING IS PRAYER

Susan Phillips, author of *The Cultivated Life* and professor of sociology and Christianity, tells us, "Through listening, relationship is cultivated and refreshment received...Sometimes graced listening takes place directly through solitary prayer with God, and sometimes it is shared with people." In a contemplative listening course Susan teaches, students write about a time they were listened to. Doing so, she writes, "something about the quality of the listening touched their hearts."

Today's prayer is inspired by the One Word Prayer, *LISTEN*. Return to a moment you felt listened to. See Jesus there, loving and listening to you, through the heart of a friend. Write your story as prayer.

The Time I Was Listened To

TODAY'S BELOVED CHALLENGE

Listen to Relaxing Sounds in Nature
(Recorded or Live)
Reinvigorate your spirit.

What's your favorite sound in nature? Stop and listen. Enjoy God's restorative sounds in nature today. (If it's too cold outside, you can play recorded nature sounds. You can find free collections available on popular music streaming services.)

SOUL CARE TRAIL NOTES

Listening to Sounds in Nature Recovers Your Good Mood

The continual noises of modern-day life—people talking, traffic, open-cubicle offices, TV, buzzing updates from smartphones—elevate stress hormones and increases anxiety. But research at Pennsylvania State found that *simply listening to sounds in nature recovers your positive mood*—better than hearing the same nature sounds with added sounds of voices and cars.

Another Swedish study found relaxing sounds of nature, whether *recorded or live*—like birds singing, ocean waves, rain—lowers stress hormone levels and shifts the brain into a relaxed state faster than without them. So go outside to hear sounds of nature or play recorded sounds indoors. You'll feel better.

Inspired

Do less and be present. Dare to be inspired.

God treasures who you are today.
Not who you will become tomorrow.

You are His Beloved.
You belong to Him. As you are.

"Your mercies are new every morning. Great is your faithfulness." LAMENTATIONS 3:23

"For the love of Christ compels us." 2 CORINTHIANS 5:14

"What day is it?" asked Winnie the Pooh.

"It's today," squeaked Piglet.

"My favorite day," said Pooh.   A. A. MILNE

I had never baked chicken before.

If you wanted your chicken stir-fried or stewed in soup, no sweat. I've paid my dues cooking as sous-chef under my Chinese mom growing up. I can tackle a whole chicken with cleaver, giblets, and all. But I'd never baked one in the oven before. Until I married a guy who loved barbecue chicken.

I wanted to surprise my one-week-new groom and greet Eric at the door after work—with a hug and the scent of his favorite meal baking. I read the recipe.

Brush olive oil on the chicken . . . Stick it in the oven. Easy enough. What threw me off wasn't the prep.

Bake forty minutes. My husband was due home in twenty minutes.

There was no way I could shorten the time. *Wait a minute . . . Maybe I could!* The directions called for an oven temperature of 325 degrees. I solved the problem by cutting my baking time in half—by turning up the temperature to 500 degrees.

With a sigh of relief, I set my egg timer and hurried to jump in the shower—when I was interrupted by the ear-piercing shrill of the smoke alarm. I jolted to the kitchen in my towel, leaving behind a wet trail and flung the oven door open.

Black smoke fumed out. *Oh. My. Gosh.* I forgot even paper bursts into flames at Fahrenheit 451. The chicken was definitely done.

Cooking isn't the only area in my life I've tried to hurry up time. *Waiting for an answered prayer—for God's plans to come to fruition—I try to help God out by making things happen faster.* So I turn up the heat and double up on commitment, passion, and planning.

But I end up getting burned out. To a crisp. Joy and peace go up in flames. Relationships get scorched.

What happens is I'm no longer present. I'm so preoccupied by what I want to happen or what I'm afraid will happen tomorrow. *I miss out on what God has for me today.* We need to be *reinspired.*

Do you ever feel burned out? Like there's just too much to do and not enough time? And yet, having checked your boxes, you lie awake at night, feeling disconnected from your heart?

Be Inspired: Do Less. Be Here Now.

It's tempting to strive and make things happen *now*. It's sometimes hard to stay present. We're so afraid of not doing enough, we adopt the strategy of doing too much. But what really satisfies our souls?

> *"It is in vain that you rise up early and go late to rest, eating the bread of anxious toil; for he gives to his beloved even in his sleep."*   PSALM 127:2

We become so preoccupied by the questions of tomorrow, *we miss out on the beauty, relationships, and experiences God longs to rejuvenate us with today.*

God understands. God reinspires us with a new vision to live as the Beloved.

Do less and be present. Be here now. *Dare to be inspired.*

READ GOD'S STORY

Manna. "What is it?" was the name the Israelites gave to the daily bread that fell down from heaven. "What is it?" we whisper, looking at our limited time, resources, and opportunities. Draw near as God invites us to a new way of living.

"This is what the Lord has commanded,
'Gather of it every man as much as he should eat...'

Some gathered much and some little.

When they measured it with an omer,
he who had gathered much had no excess,
and he who had gathered little had no lack."

EXODUS 16:16–18

This way of gathering is a beautiful way of life for us to experience today.

Gather—just what you need now.
Gather—only what you need today.
Leave the rest.
God will send fresh manna tomorrow again. For you.

Grace and Love Today

Dare to enjoy whatever beauty, rest, or peace—whether emotional, financial, or physical provision—that God's prepared for you *today*. Don't wait until you've done more to start living and loving. God longs to strengthen your soul with His love *today*. He will have more grace ready for you again tomorrow.

"Your mercies are new every morning. Great is your
faithfulness."

LAMENTATIONS 3:23

Let go of whatever lies beyond your heart's reach for now. Trust that when tomorrow comes, God will inspire you with new words, opportunities, wisdom, or courage—to navigate any conversation, decision, dream, or unexpected trial and pain.

Don't compare. What you gather will look different from what your neighbors gather. *Whether we gather a little or a lot— God will still bless us equally, as we need in the end.* You are beautifully treasured and uniquely celebrated.

God's provision is not given according to your efforts, but already lovingly set aside in His heart for you. Grace can't be lost, destroyed, or earned. But you must take time to receive it, friends. We are His Beloved.

☞ God's Whispers to You

Beloved,
Gather just what you need for today.
Let go of what needs to be let go.
Only do what my love compels you to do.

Let me be your today and your tomorrow.
I will give you what you need for this journey. I promise.
My mercies are new every day. I will be faithful.
Make my love be yours today.
Do less and be present. Dare to be inspired.

☞ A Prayer for Today: Give Me Courage to Live Inspired

"Your mercies are new every morning. Great is your faithfulness."
LAMENTATIONS 3:23

"For the love of Christ compels us."   2 CORINTHIANS 5:14

Dear Jesus,
Change my heart and my schedule.

Make my heart be more like yours.
Level it to the ground, if that's what it takes.

I want to do less and gather only what I need right now.
To live inspired rather than burned out.
Help me rebuild a new life that is compelled by your love today
and stop being a slave to what could happen tomorrow.

I am here now. Gather me close to your heart once again.
Amen.

Dare to change your schedule. Take your rightful place as God's Beloved.

Let God's love compel how you fill it. Or not.

As for my 500-degree chicken? I scraped off the char and smothered it thick with BBQ sauce. My sweet husband vigorously chewed on dried-out, cardboard-like chicken.

"Just curious, honey," Eric said midway. "What did you put in the chicken?"

"It's uh...my secret sauce." I quickly changed the subject. Later that night, I confessed. I promised never to use my secret sauce again.

Give Yourself Permission: Make time to be inspired. Do less. Quit one or more things completely. Especially if you're doing something out of guilt or fear. Use that time you've garnered to enjoy living and loving, compelled by God's love.

REFLECT ON YOUR STORY

1. *What can you do less of and be more present? What is one thing you can quit?*

2. *What or who is standing between you and a "daily-manna"–inspired life?*

3. *What One Word speaks to you today?*

PRAY & REST

A SIMPLE PRACTICE: YOUR *TODAY* PRAYER

Pray for God's love to compel what you choose to do today. Author and missionary Elisabeth Elliot shares her wisdom: "Today is mine. God still owns tomorrow. If we really have too much to do. Let us submit the list to him and ask him which items we must delete. When you don't know what to do next, just do the thing in front of you."

Today's One Word Prayer is *INSPIRED*. *Jesus, as I quiet my heart and lift my list to you today, I feel inspired to do this next thing and delete these:*

— 🖉 🖉 🖉 —

TODAY'S BELOVED CHALLENGE

Create a Space for Me Time

*Decorate or declutter a space for your soul to breathe—
a favorite chair or quiet corner.*

The present moment matters. Let God's love touch you
again. Be inspired.

**SOUL CARE
TRAIL
NOTES**

Declutter a Small Space for Yourself and Get Inspired

Juggling too many to-do's causes burnout, but so does physical clutter. Similar to multitasking, clutter overloads your senses, causing you to feel stressed, impairing memory and creativity.

A UCLA study concluded clutter impacts your mood and self-esteem—leaving people feeling guilty for projects undone and money spent on purchases unused. Stress hormones spiked with the presence of clutter. Women who described their homes as "cluttered" with "unfinished projects" were more depressed, fatigued, showing *higher levels of the stress hormone cortisol* than those whose homes felt "restful" and "restorative."

By decluttering even a small space for your Me Time—to read, be creative, or rest—you'll spark inspiration again. The amount of stress was shown to be directly proportional to the amount of things people owned. Get inspired. Launch a decluttering marathon and purge what doesn't spark joy.

Hope

Re-architect a new life with me. Dare to hope again.

God's love is a lighthouse of hope
for your heart to rest and return home to,
as many times as you need.

Your Heavenly Father whispers,
I see and cherish you.
Re-architect a new life with me.
Dare to hope again.

*"Yes, my soul, find rest in God; my hope comes
from him."*   PSALM 62:5

✑ ✑ ✑

"Life takes us to unexpected places...Love brings us home." UNKNOWN

My friends Thomas and Marie have just adopted a baby girl from China. What's unique is this: She had been abandoned and passed over many times because she has special needs. Until one day, this little girl became *chosen*.

She suddenly flew to a new country—with a daddy and a mommy who have given her a new name. Beatrix has a new home. She *belongs* to a real family.

But like other children institutionalized by a round-robin of changing caregivers at the orphanage, Beatrix needs something very important she missed out on: emotional bonding to parents who love her. *She is on a new journey to become the Beloved.*

Beatrix is learning she doesn't have to battle for attention. She doesn't need to perform to be loved, to catch a caregiver's attention. She doesn't have to cry alone in the dark anymore. Her father will hold her and her mother will comfort her.

Beatrix is learning her voice matters. She is taking on a new identity. Until she adjusts to this new safe reality, her blood pressure is spiked high. She doesn't look anxious, but her body does not lie. She is very stressed. It will take months before she learns through time and new, daily experiences that love won't leave.

We are a lot like Beatrix, learning to trust that love will grow and stay. We are each on a journey to grow into our new identity as God's Beloved, to respond to a new name and venture out into new experiences.

Will God really come through for me? Can I really dare

to be optimistic about my future, my dreams, and who I'm becoming?

We all need hope to come alive again.

Dare to Hope Again

Is your soul missing this renewed hope, too? We all need hope that our voices matter—that there is a better tomorrow for us. That our past is moving behind us as a daughter who is no longer overlooked, but cherished. That God hears our cries and celebrates our new discoveries.

Like Beatrix, learning to speak a new language, we are pilgrims learning a new language to dwell in a new land. *This new language of the soul—in this new land of God's love—is hope. We need the heartbeat of hope to breathe in us again.*

I once told God I didn't want any more hope. Hope had died one too many times, and I couldn't take losing it again. *Just tell me what to do and I'll do it.*

Hope complicates things. It was easier to just stay in survival mode and do life as maintenance. Maybe that's what an orphan whispers to herself.

But God's hope rescues us and brings us to a new reality: We are no longer orphans. Our destinies are no longer left to what this world, our past or our weaknesses say about us. We are God's Beloved. Dare to hope again.

What new experiences would you dare explore if you had hope renewed? Move beyond the round-robin of noisy voices of our critics, including our own voices.

The world celebrates people who go out and make things happen. This is how the world gains hope. Hope is a goal we accomplish, and our schedules reflect this. *Jesus offers us a radically different vision of what fuels hope: his love.*

Hope comes alive when someone loves us irrevocably.

Intimately. Continuously. Hear Jesus whisper, *I am your hope. My love will grow and stay.*

We are no longer trapped by our need to be useful, important or gifted. *What fuels hope is love.* We were made to be loved.

READ GOD'S STORY

To keep hope alive, Jesus invites us to a new way of living.

> *"Just as the Father has loved me,*
> *I have also loved you.*
> *Abide in my love."*
>
> JOHN 15:9

The word "abide" doesn't sound impressive. Yet, it's the one action Jesus reveals as his secret to a fruitful life. *What does "abide" actually mean?* I wondered.

The Greek word for "abide" means "*to dwell*" and "*to be held.*"

Not only does "abide" mean to be held—*but to be continually held.* The active and continuous verb tense reveals something amazing: *We are called to actively make a home—to dwell continually—in God's love.*

To continually learn to be at home in your belovedness makes a difference. God wants you experience a new kind of home in you—one in which the Holy Spirit fills you with hope, joy and peace. Hope is the oxygen that your soul breathes. Hope reenergizes you with an inner, flowing power to trust God will take care of you, even in the midst of your weakness and the trials of everyday life.

> *"May the God of hope fill you with all joy and peace*
> *as you trust in him,*
> *so that you may overflow with hope*
> *by the power of the Holy Spirit."*
>
> ROMANS 15:13

We are invited to re-architect a new kind of life, by creating a schedule optimized to continually be replenished daily by God's love—and extend this gift to others.

It may not be easy. *But Jesus doesn't expect perfection. He treasures your faith.*

☞ *God's Whispers to You*

Beloved,
My love is a lighthouse of hope
for your heart to rest and return home to,
as many times as you need today.

Dare to hope again. Move out with me today.
You are no longer an orphan. I call you beloved daughter.
I choose you. My love is irrevocable. Always.

Re-architect a new life with me.
Change your schedule with hope.
Dare to hope again.

☞ *A Prayer for Today:* *Give Me Courage to Hope Again*

"Yes, my soul, find rest in God; my hope comes from him."   PSALM 62:5

Dear Jesus,
Hope is a new soul language for me.
I thought I could live without too much of it
and just soldier on.

But you've changed all that now. You love me.

Renew my hope in you again.
Fill me with joy and peace.
Empower me with your Holy Spirit.

Give me courage to re-architect my life with hope,
Give me a new vision to live life as your beloved daughter.
Thank you, Heavenly Father.
Amen.

Whatever you're facing, God can renew your hope. Hope matters. You matter.

Give Yourself Permission: Cast a new vision of hope for yourself and what tomorrow can bring. Surround yourself with experiences—and spend time with people—that make you feel loved and feel hope in your heart rise again.

REFLECT ON YOUR STORY

1. *If you re-architect your life with hope, what would it look like? How is God calling you to dare to hope again?*

2. *What One Word speaks to you today?*

PRAY & REST

A SIMPLE PRACTICE: PRAYER FOR HOPE

Today's One Word Prayer is *HOPE*. When life wears us down, we stop hoping to avoid disappointment. But God says never give up hope. "Hope will not lead to disappointment. For we know how dearly God loves us" (Romans 5:5).

Devotional writer Roy Lessin shares in *Today Is Your Best Day*, "Through prayer, God has something new for you every day. The love God has for you and your love for Him work together to make this your best day."

Jesus, renew my hope in Your plans / Your love for me in this area of my life . . .

TODAY'S BELOVED CHALLENGE

Wear Your Favorite Color

Channel the power of colors in your outfit today.
Elevate your mood.

You are God's gift to this world, architected to be daily loved.

Wearing Color Improves Your Mood

When we are renewed by hope, the day feels different. The colors we surround ourselves with also affect our mood. Scientists have proven colors change moods and affect brain function. A University of British Columbia study found rooms painted in blue boosts creative tasks more than red. Room color also affects how much people eat, with yellow's sunshine mood increasing appetite.

Just as interior designers use colors to create a different mood to a room, wearing colors can inspire, energize, or bring you calm. Try wearing a different color and see how you feel. Or take a dare. Paint your walls with color.

Here are some colors and what they signify. Enjoy experimenting!

Pink: gentle, calming, happiness
—associated with love, if you're opening your heart
Green: tranquility, stress-reducing, refreshing
—associated with nature, if you're feeling overwhelmed
Blue: peaceful, calming, creative

—associated with blue skies, if you're navigating change

Orange: energetic, happy, enthusiasm

—associated with positivity, if you're feeling social/inspired

Yellow: joy, cheerful, laughter

—associated with sunshine, if you're wanting a pick-me-up

DAY 33

Blossom

You are perfect in my eyes. Dare to blossom.

Move out in my love.
You are perfect in my eyes.
You can blossom today. As is.

"I will heal your wandering. I will love you freely.
You will be like dew to Israel, you will blossom like
the lily."   HOSEA 14:4–5

❦ ❦ ❦

"Don't ask yourself what the world needs; ask yourself what makes you come alive. And then go do that. Because what the world needs is people who have come alive." DR. HOWARD THURMAN

I used to tell myself, "I have to stop being a perfectionist!"

Can anyone else hear the irony of those words? One of the biggest traps I often fall into is the notion that I can get rid of perfectionism.

If only I had more confidence in myself...

If only I could let go of the past...

If only I trusted God more...

If only...

All this *If-Only* thinking accomplished only one thing: It prevented me from stepping forward and doing what God had inspired my heart to do as His Beloved.

God isn't waiting for us to *be better*. God is longing to *love us deeper*—more than we have ever dared to imagine.

God whispers: *Move out in my love. You are perfect in my eyes. Blossom today. As you are.*

I have gone through a lot of restarts in my life. One thing I've found consistent: The voice of perfectionism always tries to stop me. The newer the step, the louder the criticisms of perfectionism hisses.

It's become so predictable that I came to a startling conclusion: The pull toward perfectionism isn't going away. On this side of heaven, these critical voices can't be annihilated completely.

But I've also found *a more powerful truth*: The voice of God dares me to *step forward anyway, because I am more loved than my imperfections.*

Part of being human is experiencing our weaknesses. But it doesn't have to control the choices we make.

Dare to Blossom

You and I don't have to wait until we are free from perfectionism to start taking new steps. *Like a rose petal moved by the sunlight of God's love, we can blossom today as God's created us.*

I began taking my sights off my imperfections (knowing they were still there) and did a word study in Scripture on "perfect" and "love" through the Bible. I began taking the **Love Dare**.

I'd done a pretty good job of listening to the voices of perfectionism. I decided to try an experiment for my soul. *What would happen if I started siding with the voice of God's love?*

Using the nuggets dug up from God's word, I challenged myself—*as a dare*—to make choices that reflected my trust in God's love for me, rather than how I felt about myself.

The Love Dare

Whenever I get to a fork in the road, I dare to:

1. Stop making decisions based on three things:

    fear of failure, mistakes, or others' opinions of me.

2. Take the step that reflects only *one thing*:

    God's unconditional love for me.

    The Love Dare is based on this key verse:

    "We rely on the love God has for us. God is love.

There is no fear in love.
But perfect love drives out fear."   1 JOHN 4:16, 18

READ GOD'S STORY

Top Five Lies of Perfectionism and Five Truths to Help Your Soul Blossom

Do you find perfectionism holding you back on your new journey of faith? As I took the *Love Dare*, I found whispers of rest to combat the *Top Five Lies of Perfectionism: Five Truths to Help Your Soul Blossom.*

Lie #1: I'm not good enough.
Truth #1: So what? God loves what I'm doing anyway!

"If I must boast, I will boast of the things that show my weakness . . . God's power works best in my weakness."
           2 CORINTHIANS 11:30, 12:9

Lie #2: It's too late.
Truth #2: It's never too late. God saves the best for last!

"Everyone brings out the choice wine first and then the cheaper wine after the guests have had too much to drink; but you have saved the best till now."   JOHN 2:10

Lie #3: Why bother starting if I can't finish?
Truth #3: I don't know how long this will take. But if God's in it, I'll make it!

"Being confident of this, that he who began a good work in you will carry it on to completion until the day of Christ Jesus."
           PHILIPPIANS 1:6

Lie #4: People won't like me.

Truth #4: Not everyone will. It will hurt, but God still thinks I'm wonderful!

"It is a very small thing that I may be examined by you, or by any human court; in fact, I do not even examine myself . . . but the one who examines me is the Lord."

1 CORINTHIANS 4:3–4

Lie #5: People will hurt me.

Truth #5: Even if that's true, hurt won't be my end. God's love for me still wins in the end!

"You intended to harm me, but God intended it for good."

GENESIS 50:20

Take the *Love Dare* when you find yourself at a fork in the road today. Perfectionism can tug at us many times during the day—but remember God's love will never grow tired or weary.

"He who keeps you will not slumber."   PSALM 121:4

God's love goes beyond our limits. And nothing— *not even perfectionism*—can keep God's love from you. The voice of God dares us to step forward, because you are more loved than any imperfections.

✑ God's Whispers to You

Beloved,
What others call flaws,
I see a beautiful doorway into your heart,
to love you deeper and make them all my own.

I see the real you,
that I created with beauty and great affection.

Move out in my love today.
You are perfect in my eyes.
Blossom today. As is.

✍ *A Prayer for Today:*
To Overcome Perfectionism—Give Me
Courage to Blossom

"We rely on the love God has for us. God is love.
There is no fear in love. But perfect love drives out fear."

1 JOHN 4:16, 18

Dear Jesus,
Give me courage to blossom today.
To rely on your love for me,
instead of what others say about me
or what I say about myself.

Free me to move out
to be and do as you've inspired me.

When I see my imperfections,
strengthen my heart with the truth.

Drop fresh words of love on my soul again, sweet like rain,
and I will blossom with your hand in mine today.
Amen.

If you feel hesitant to go for the blessings God's put on your heart, don't hold yourself back because of history or shortcomings in your view. Dare to blossom. Just as you are.

Give Yourself Permission: Do things afraid or imperfectly. Don't compare. Turn your back on your critics and follow Jesus ahead. Do as God prompts you right now. *Loved.*

REFLECT ON YOUR STORY

1. *Which of the Five Whispers of Truth inspires you to blossom?*

2. *How is perfectionism holding you back? What areas is God encouraging you to step forward in?*

3. *What One Word speaks to you today?*

PRAY & REST

A SIMPLE PRACTICE: GOD'S LOVE NOTES—LIES AND TRUTHS

My friend Lysa TerKeurst, author of *Uninvited*, wrote a beautiful prayer: "Help me to rest in the truth of Psalm 86:13, 'Great is your love toward me.' You already see the ways I will fall short and mess up. But right now, I consciously tuck Your whisper of absolute love for me into the deepest part of my heart. I recognize Your love for me is not based on my performance...shortcomings and all. But what's most amazing is the Savior of the world would desire a few minutes with me this morning. Lord, help me to forever remember what a gift it is to sit with You like this. In Jesus' name, Amen."

For today's prayer, sit with Jesus and receive God's Love Notes. Contemplate "Great is your love toward me." What lies are you listening to? What are God's whispers of truth to replace them?

Lies of Perfectionism	*God's Love Notes—Truths*

Write your BLOSSOM prayer here...

1.   1.

2.   2.

3.   3.

TODAY'S BELOVED CHALLENGE

Take a Digital Break

Turn off your phone and computer for two hours.
Enjoy an experience
that makes you feel happy and alive.

God's love makes *you* perfect in His eyes. He is yours.

SOUL CARE TRAIL NOTES

Turn Off Social Media and Be Happier

Perfectionism allows no room for mistakes or for exploration and creativity. Yet, studies show that self-criticism—being hard on ourselves—actually eliminates motivation, reducing goal completion. University of California researcher Sonja Lyubomirsky found that unhappy people spend hours comparing themselves to others and care about results. Happy people didn't compare themselves with anyone.

The more time people spent on Facebook and social media, the more they felt dissatisfied, depressed, or anxious. People avoid sharing negative feelings, so what you see isn't real but tweaked.

To increase your feelings of happiness and reduce anxiety, *choose real experiences* rather than looking at social media. Research found that experiences make people happier and give people a greater sense of vitality—"feeling alive." Happiness enjoyed during the experience carried lasting benefits. Simply by recalling the memory sparked happy brain activity, elevating good mood.

PART SIX

Shining as the Beloved

✦ ✦ ✦

Celebrate Your Calling:
Be God's Radiant Light

The last movement on your journey to be the Beloved
invites you to celebrate your calling as God's radiant light.

Jesus whispers,
You are my Greatest Treasure.
You were made to shine.

The concluding devotionals point you
to celebrate all the ways you can uniquely shine—
to embrace your gifts, find your voice,
and reignite your *First Love* for God.

May you be inspired to find your spark
and be who God created you to be.

"You will shine like stars in the sky."　　PHILIPPIANS 2:15

❧ ❧ ❧

Light

Shine bright. You are my Light.

When you wonder if you are beautiful,
Jesus whispers,
Like the stars silently moving across the night sky,
You are special. Sparkle.
Shine bright. You are my Light.

"You will shine like stars in the sky."   PHILIPPIANS 2:15

"Never lose an opportunity of seeing anything beautiful. Beauty is God's handwriting. Welcome it...drink it in...a cup of blessing." CHARLES KINGSLEY

As I shared when we began this forty-day journey, I grew up in Silicon Valley, which meant I had trouble seeing the stars. As a child, looking up into the night sky through my bedroom curtains, I often saw clouds move in gray silhouettes. If I was lucky, I'd see a few dots standing still.

Were they part of the Big Dipper? I would just have to imagine they were. Sometimes, I'd squint really hard and suspend belief to convince myself, *Yes. That star is twinkling.*

Light pollution. It's what happens when the shimmering river of stars in the sky is lost to artificial light—reflecting from streetlights and man-made sources—falling where it's not intended, excessively brightening the sky. One by one, the stars fade and disappear—*not because they're not twinkling*—but because they're lost in the glare from overlit urban areas, focusing our attention on everything manufactured, marketing signage, and buildings.

In the same way, our fast-paced lives creates noise pollution for our souls. Do you find it difficult to hear God's loving voice and feel as special, cherished, and beautiful as you truly are? God is whispering—*Shine your light.*

You Are God's Light

Sometimes we're inspired to experience something beautiful God puts on our hearts, to actually step out and sparkle, to make space to feed our souls and shine. But like the stars covered by the clutter of light pollution, our confidence fades, as we often adopt language that applies to products to our souls.

We are told we need to cultivate a following, craft a beautiful feed, continuously improve ourselves to get more done in less time, with greater innovation and fewer mistakes, in order to reinvent ourselves to be worthy of likes and shares.

But this is not how a beautiful life is experienced or lived. *You were created to shine brightly.* When the sun sets in the beauty of the dark, we see the beautiful planets and stars that God ignited thousands of years ago—so we can see them twinkle today, to a steady heavenly heartbeat.

You were created with this beauty in mind—not to ignore the dark or erase it from your life—but to give light to the darkness.

God placed a beautiful, natural light in you that no amount of clutter can destroy: His *love.* He whispers—*You are special. You are beautiful. Sparkle. Shine. You are my light.*

READ GOD'S STORY

Imagine yourself now, among the disciples who climbed a hill far from the city rush, to sit close with Jesus. Listen as he speaks to you now:

"You are the light of the world. A city set on a hill cannot be hidden.

No one lights a lamp and then puts it under a basket.

Instead, a lamp is placed on a stand, where it gives light to everyone in the house.

Let your light shine before men in such a way that they may see your good works, and glorify your Father who is in heaven."

MATTHEW 5:14–16

The world needs the light your voice brings. You weren't created to be covered up by a basket or anything else man-made. You were created with beauty to be shared—to be placed out in the open. To shine and sparkle.

Would you ever tell a child to hide her crayon drawings or stop singing when she's dancing in the sun? We celebrate the sparkle of creativity and beauty in our children, placing their drawings on our fridge much as a Monet would be hung in a museum. *How much more our Father in Heaven celebrates and proudly wants you to shine!*

Whether it's through the song echoing in your heart—as you hug your children, listen to your friend, or prepare a meal for those in need, tutor others, or share the broken, healing parts of your story—it is time for you to step out to shine *your* light to other people. So others no longer have to hide in the dark.

You are worthy to shine with Jesus—simply because He breathes in you.

✏ *God's Whispers to You*

Beloved,
You are my light.
It breaks my heart to see you hide,
all the beautiful things I've ignited in your heart.

When I see you quiet, at rest,
every dream you've whispered,
even the tears you've swallowed,
they echo the light of my love for you.

I call you beautiful. You are wonderfully made.
You are special. Sparkle.
Shine bright. You are my light.

✒ A Prayer for Today: Be God's Light and Shine Bright

"You will shine like stars in the sky."   PHILIPPIANS 2:15

Dear Jesus,
Give me courage to shine for you.
I want to step out from what covers me,
and share the light you've given me,
during the happy and dark times.

Be thou my vision,
So others no longer have to journey alone.
Warm my heart by the light of your love
so that my sparkle will ignite others
to shine bright with you and for you, too.
Amen.

When you see darkness more than light, faith will shine God's light through you. Just like the beautiful stars God flung into the sky, we won't be able to tell the difference between one moment of faith and another moment of pain. In His eyes, they are all the same.

We will all sparkle, twinkling in God's whispers of love for us.

Give Yourself Permission: Do things that bring light and beauty into your day. Enjoy places that inspire your spirit to sparkle. Cultivate interests that make you feel beautiful. Take care of your body, your skin, and your emotional well-being. Shine in your unique way.

REFLECT ON YOUR STORY

1. *How is God calling you to step out and shine?*

2. *What are some interests, rhythms, practices, or relationships you can incorporate into your day to feel more beautiful in your body or shine in your personality, gifting, or passion?*

3. *What is the light God placed in you, to inspire or encourage others?*

4. *What One Word speaks to you today?*

PRAY & REST

A SIMPLE PRACTICE: PRAY FOR LIGHT

Today, we pray God's light to shine in our hearts. Hannah Whitall Smith, author and activist for the women's suffrage movement, wrote: "Put together all the tenderest love you know of... multiply it by infinity, and you will begin perhaps to have some faint glimpses of the love and grace of God."

Reflect on today's One Word Prayer, *LIGHT.* Light conveys different meanings in scripture. How does light speak to you?

Faithful care (Psalm 43:3)   *Rescue* (Psalm 27:1)
God's presence (Exodus 13:21)   *Hope* (1 Peter 1:19)
Truth (Ephesians 5:13)   *Guidance* (Psalm 119:105)
Jesus, shine your Light in this area of my life....

Jesus, help me shine your Light to others through me in this way...

TODAY'S BELOVED CHALLENGE

Soak Up Some Sunshine
Step Outside and Take a Break
Go for a stroll or relax in the sun.
Sunlight keeps your body and soul happy.

Enjoy the warmth of the sun. Return energized. Shine brightly.

SOUL CARE TRAIL NOTES

Soak Up Sunshine—Vitamins for a Happy Body and Soul

Just as God's love brightens our spirit, soaking up sunshine makes the soul and body happy. Research shows our bodies to respond to sunlight by releasing a burst of serotonin, a natural happy hormone, that boosts our mood whenever we are outside in sunshine. That's why light therapy lifts symptoms of seasonal depression.

Getting just five to fifteen minutes of sunshine on your arms, hands, and face can give you enough vitamin D to enjoy the boosting benefits of the sun: lowering blood pressure, improving memory, easing depression, and improving sleep by setting your body's normal circadian (sleep/awake) rhythm. By stepping out in sunshine, you also get vitamins for the soul: God's love for you found in the beauty in nature. God cares for you.

❦ ❦ ❦

First Love

Glow bright. Let me be your First Love.

If you wonder if love could ever
be uncomplicated again,
Jesus whispers,
Don't worry about anything.
Just let me love you. Glow bright.
Let me be your First Love again.

"I am my beloved's and my beloved is mine."

SONG OF SOLOMON 6:3

✐ ✐ ✐

> "You wake…and—for a moment—you *know*: beyond all
> the noise and the gestures, the only real thing, love's calm
> unwavering flame in the half-light of an early dawn."
>
> DAG HAMMARSKJÖLD

The moment seemed perfect. He was holding me close as I sank into his embrace. I could see the stars twinkling above us across the sky as I laid my head on his shoulder.

We were saying good night before I would get in my car to return home. Eric just made us dinner at his apartment. Baked chicken with teriyaki sauce, with edamame for appetizers. I was impressed. We'd just started dating a couple weeks after meeting at church, e-mailing each other every day for a month.

After dinner, we snuggled on the couch looking through photo albums, swapping notes on where Eric traveled during his early days with the Army, and where I was, a twenty-something, newly graduated California girl. I felt so close to him, hearing his sandy-soft voice tell stories as he laughed, reliving memories through each other's tales.

As we held each other in the parking lot that quiet summer night, it happened. Slowly, tenderly, he nestled me in, even closer. To kiss me.

But I was afraid. What if I liked him more than he liked me? How serious was this really going to be? I didn't want him to think I didn't want to kiss him. But I had kissed too many frogs, and my heart just couldn't handle any more memories of kisses that never stayed.

"I'm sorry," I turned away, stumbling for what to say next.

"What is it?" Eric asked, a soft silhouette in the night.

"No, I want to, but…" I didn't want to say too much, but fearful I wasn't saying enough. "I'm sorry," I said again. "It's complicated." I felt my chances for love slip away as more words tumbled out of me. Like a scratch skipping across your favorite LP as it plays, I was ruining the moment.

"Sshh..." Eric whispered, gathering me close into his gaze. "You don't have to worry about a thing. Just let me love you." Then he simply held me.

We stood there, lingering in the moment, before he tucked me in my car and I drove into the night irrevocably changed.

And that was the very moment I knew he was the one.

The Defining Moment

Sometimes, there is a defining moment when you realize you are truly, honestly loved. Those defining moments happen when you reveal something about yourself that is utterly vulnerable and raw, when you place your heart into someone's hands, not knowing if they will take you or leave you. But vulnerability is the doorway to the very soul of intimacy—to be known, accepted, and loved.

All of us who have been named by God, who have heard His whispers, have such a Determine-the-Relationship (DTR) moment in our story with Him. *Your First Love Moment.*

> "But you walked away from your first love—why?
> Turn back. Recover your dear early love."
>
> REVELATION 2:4–5

Do you remember your First Love Moment is that spark that first lit your heart when you heard God's voice and you knew *He was the very one* who loves you—when you gave yourself fully to Him and tasted the joy of experiencing His presence? This is the defining moment that God continually calls us to return—*Let me be your First Love again.*

You Are God's First Love

As you revisit stories that have surfaced during this forty-day journey through God's Whispers of Rest, have you caught a glimpse of who you have always been in God's arms—*as His Beloved?* Take a moment now to allow the many scenes from your life flash across your mind.

Invite Jesus to sit next to you in that secret place within you; show him the memories that mean the most to you, as you've journeyed through them together—whether they have caused you hurt and confusion or brought you great joy, beauty, and peace.

Your feelings may be complicated, but it's becoming clearer. Just like that moment your eyes adjust to the twinkle of stars at night, you see how much God *really and truly loves you* in a deeper way. You want to open your heart to Him again, to let Him love you now anew.

Remember God is your First Love and you are His. Glow brightly.

READ GOD'S STORY

Listen to God's whispers of love to Israel as words spoken to you, to achingly draw her back to Himself, to return to the passion and intimacy of *First Love*:

> *"Therefore, I will now allure her,*
> *and bring her into the wilderness,*
> *and speak tenderly to her...*
>
> *I will make the Valley of [Trouble] a door of hope.*
>
> *There she shall respond as in the days of her youth,*
> *as at the time when she came out of the land of Egypt.*

*On that day, says the Lord, you will call me, 'My
husband.'*

I will make for you a covenant *on that day.
I will make you* lie down in safety.

And I will take you to be my wife forever…
in steadfast love and in mercy.

I will betroth you to me in faithfulness;

and you will know *the Lord."*   HOSEA 2:14, 15B–16, 18–20

When it says we will "know" the Lord, the Hebrew root word *yada* means to *experience* God and *to reveal oneself.* It is the same *intimate knowing* when a man and a woman make love on their wedding night, as in Genesis 4:1 when "Adam *knew* Eve his wife and she conceived."

It is also unexpected and intriguing to hear God use the word "allure," which, translated from the Hebrew word *Pathah,* means "to persuade, attract or entice."

Hear God *alluring* the one He loves, speaking tenderly to her, taking her for His wife in love. *Does this kind of tender and intimate language surprise you? How do you notice yourself reacting to it?*

Can you see yourself as the object of God's love, as the one He wants to allure? Do you ever feel that your relationship with God has become weary or faded—yet you remember how you once glowed, when you responded to God's voice and felt God responding to you?

Respond to God's Longing

Knowing that God is longing to respond to you, can you share with Him about that now? Stop. *Take a moment to write and talk with God, as your Intimate Love and Confidant.*

> *Dear Jesus, This is how I feel, knowing that you are longing to respond to me . . .*

✐ *God's Whispers to You*

Beloved,
I've always longed to love you the way
you've always dreamed of being loved,
in the way I've always intended for you.

There will never come a time
I'll stop whispering words of love to you.

Come back to me. To your first love.
Let me turn your valley of troubles into a door of hope.

Don't worry about anything.
Just let me love you.
Glow bright. Let me be your First Love.

A Prayer for Today:
Return to Your First Love

"I am my beloved's and my beloved is mine."

SONG OF SOLOMON 6:3

Dear Jesus,
It's complicated. I'm complicated.
You see how my affections have faded.
Yet you take me in your arms now
and you call me yours.

Love my heart back to life again.
I want to know you more deeply.
I give myself to you right now.

Light the fire of our first love.
Then, I'll glow again.
Thank you for loving me so truly. I love you.
Amen.

Give Yourself Permission: Be honest about the distance between the two of you. Share any doubts or complicated feelings with Jesus. He'll draw you back. Retell yourself the love story of how you and Jesus met. *Enjoy whatever God inspires you with to rekindle your affections and feel close to Him again.*

REFLECT ON YOUR STORY

1. *What was it like, when you first fell in love with someone? How did it feel?*

2. *Recall a defining moment in your relationship with Jesus. When did his love for you became a personal experience?*

3. *What are things you can do to renew your First Love for Jesus?*

PRAY & REST

A SIMPLE PRACTICE: "HOW WE MET"–RETELL YOUR LOVE STORY

Brennan Manning, author and Franciscan priest, prayed in *Souvenirs of Solitude*, "Lord, when I feel that what I'm doing is insignificant and unimportant, help me to remember that everything I do is significant and important in your eyes, because you love me." Is there a special song, place, object, scent, or activity you were experiencing—that created those first moments in your Love Story with Jesus?

Today's One Word Prayer is *FIRST LOVE*. Think back now on your defining moments with God—jot notes—and let them inspire you to revisit those same songs, places, mementos, scents, or activities today or in the coming weeks. Rekindle those moments. Make plans to enjoy them again with Jesus.

Jesus, here are memories of how we met, when I came to first know you love me:

TODAY'S BELOVED CHALLENGE

Rekindle Love and Friendship
Schedule a New Experience *Date Night,
Girls' Night Out, or Mommy-and-Me Date.*

Jesus loves you. Rediscover your first love. Glow brightly.

SOUL CARE TRAIL NOTES

Rekindle Love by Enjoying New Experiences Together

Romantic love in marriage doesn't have to fade. Scientists tell us long-married couples can rekindle romantic love. How? *Try enjoying new experiences together.*

Brain science shows that new experiences activate the brain's reward system, flooding it with and norepinephrine. *Novelty*, simply doing new things together as a couple, re-creates the chemical surges of courtship. Instead of visiting the same places, reinvent your date nights; this can be as simple as trying a new restaurant, driving to a different part of town, or playing tourist, rediscovering nearby sights. Take a museum or brewery tour, or hike a new trail.

The benefits of novelty don't just apply to the married. Girls' nights out can also *strengthen friendships* when you enjoy new experiences, like doing a paint night. Single or married, parents can create new memories with their children. Eric and I love coming up with simple, local outings to take our boys as a family (we call them *Family Adventures*), deepening our bond. We also started sprinkling *Mommy-and-Me* and *Daddy-and-Me Dates* into the calendar. They're as simple as fro-yo or minigolf, which feels new for the boys to enjoy one-on-one.

꙳ ꙳ ꙳

Gift

Sparkle bright. You are my Gift.

If you feel unsure
about what you have to offer,
Jesus whispers,
You are more than enough.
There is no one like you.
Be bold. Sparkle bright.
You are my Gift.

"Fan into flame the gift of God which is in you…
For God gave us a spirit not of fear,
but of power and love and self-control."

2 TIMOTHY 1:6–7

"There is only one of you in all time; this expression is unique. It is not your business to determine how good it is, nor how it compares. It is your business to keep it yours clearly." MARTHA GRAHAM

Sometimes, you may feel small when you look at the different ways everyone may be offering a gift to the world. You see the little seed in your hand and wonder if it could ever grow into anything as beautiful as the oak tree that rests on a quiet hill.

But there is Someone who sees the light within you. That Someone dreamed of you, as He looked out into the stars He named, and He felt inspired to place a part of Himself that no one else has—in *you*. Your Heavenly Father decided to make something original and bright. *One of a kind.*

God made you. You are an original. You cannot be replaced. You uniquely reflect a part of His personality, in a way no one else can. Maybe it's the way you do things with an ease for organization or decorate a space with an eye for beauty. Maybe you create music, while someone else tells stories. Or it can be the way you deeply listen, able to give words with an intuition and insight that help others feel understood and put things in a fresh perspective. Discernment and wisdom are spiritual gifts mentioned in the Bible (see Romans 12:8–10).

No one else can offer this gift except you. Like the flowers God silently blooms in a meadow, you may not even been aware it was a gift. It gives you joy so simply, it surprises you to imagine it offering anyone else the same joy.

To find you spark again, you need to use your gifts by faith. What is a gift you may have given up on—that God longs to fan into flames in you today?

Finding Your Flow

When you use your gifts, the world becomes a peaceful place where you belong. People call it "finding your flow." But I call it *falling into the embrace of God's presence.*

The most amazing thing happens when you share your gift with others: They experience God's peace, too. Like the quiet brilliance of a fire fanned into flame in the night, rekindle the light of God's love and you'll inspire others to shine, too.

As you journey through whispers of rest, is there a gift God wants you to kindle afresh and use again? Listen now to the sweet gentle voice of the Savior who guards his gift of love in you.

> *"A crushed reed he will not break,*
> *and a fading candle he won't snuff out."* ISAIAH 42:3

READ GOD'S STORY

Jesus' words are spoken through Paul's last letter in prison to encourage his young friend Timothy—who lost his spark among the daily grind and needed to find it again. Timothy was discouraged and was tempted to be timid and retreat.

Are you feeling timid, too? Hear Paul's encouragement as written to you:

> *"Fan into flame—kindle afresh—the gift of God which*
> *is in you… For God has not given us a spirit of timidity*
> *[fear], but of power, love, and self-control.*
> *So, do not be ashamed of the testimony of the Lord."*
> 2 TIMOTHY 1:6–8

How is God calling you to fan into flames His gift—that

is alive in you? To give proof and testify that God is real and moves in you?

Don't be timid. To rekindle your gift, you need to *use* it! If you're not sure, it just means you get to explore *what it could be.*

You Are God's Gift

Different gifts are also uncovered in different seasons of your life. So it's not always the same. *The Holy Spirit is very dynamic.* The more you rest in God's love, the more you pick up gifts you once left behind or discover new ones.

Do you enjoy refreshing others through the gift of hospitality? Maybe it's your gift of encouragement, cooking a meal or brewing a cup of coffee that says *I have time for you.* Is your gift expressed in photography, teaching a child to play, creating music or art, or starting a ministry that speaks to you? The gift you have to offer can be as simple and profound as the gift of listening so someone can feel heard today. (To learn about spiritual gifts referenced in the Bible, see *Book Resources* for Day 36.)

Whatever your gifting is, fan it into flame and kindle it afresh *by feeding your passion.* As you do, you'll find *the biggest gift* God longs for you to offer *is the real you.*

Be curious. Sparkle brightly. *You* are God's gift.

✑ *God's Whispers to You*

Beloved,
My gift in you is irrevocable,
kindled by the Holy Spirit,
as a token of my pledge of love to you.

Share this gift,
as a testimony of your new identity as my Beloved.

Don't be ashamed.
Let my love catch fire in you.
There is no one like you.
Kindle afresh my gift in you. Fan it into flame.
Be bold. Sparkle bright. You are my Gift.

✍ *A Prayer for Today:*
Light Up God's Gift in You

"Fan into flame—kindle afresh—the gift of God which is in you... For God did not give us spirit of timidity [fear], but of power, love and self-control".

2 TIMOTHY 1:6–7

Dear Jesus,
Help me to be bold to shine for you again.
Relight the fire that has gone dim,
Kindle afresh the gift you've put into my heart.

Give me courage to take action today,
To use my gifts to bless others
To fan the flame by feeding my passion.
Help me to be curious, to explore any new gifts
that you're igniting in me this new season.
Amen.

Be bold. Take God's hand and together, dust off the gift He's awakening. *Be patient and protect it.* Encourage yourself to fan into flames God's gift in you.

Give Yourself Permission: Be curious. Stop overthinking. Take action. Let go of commitments that keep you from developing and expressing your gift. Explore a new gift.

REFLECT ON YOUR STORY

1. *What gifts has God put in you? What is something you like to do—a natural interest or passion—that makes you happy and brings joy to other people, too?*

2. *Who has encouraged you in your gifting—what did they say? Have you felt timid or fearful to shine? Why?*

3. *What steps can you take to feed your passion or explore your gifts?*

4. *What One Word speaks to you in today's Scripture?*

PRAY & REST

A SIMPLE PRACTICE: SEEK, FIND, AND KNOCK

Philosopher Dallas Willard, author of *Divine Conspiracy*, gives insight into rekindling prayer. "The way to get to meaningful prayer...is to start by praying for what we are truly interested in. The circle of our interests will inevitably grow in the largeness of God's love." Jesus said, "Ask and it will be given to you. Seek and you shall find. Knock and the door will be opened to you" (Luke 11:9).

For today's One Word prompt *GIFT*, ask Jesus to rekindle your desire to *ask* (get inspired), *seek* (explore and try), or *knock* (find new opportunities to use it).

Jesus, I ask you to rekindle this gift _____ in me. My ideas (brainstorm):

⌇ ⌇ ⌇

TODAY'S BELOVED CHALLENGE

Cook Something Yummy
Enjoy the therapeutic benefits of cooking.
Rekindle your soul.

I love making soup after a rough week, getting lost in the chopping and comfort of warm food. What do you enjoy cooking?

SOUL CARE TRAIL NOTES

Therapeutic Gifts of Preparing a Meal

Feeding your passion reenergizes you. Preparing a meal, as you chop and dice, refreshes your soul, too. A *Wall Street Journal* report shows that people suffering from stress and depression benefit from *cooking therapy*.

The act of prepping a meal relieves stress by clearing your mind of negative thoughts, freeing you to be present in the moment. Stress numbs us, but cooking yummy food is a nurturing, creative outlet, reawakening your senses to aromas, touch, visual delight, and sounds.

≪ ≪ ≪

Poetry

Shine brilliantly. You are my Work of Art.

Just as poetry reflects God's creativity,
Jesus invites you to be just like him.

Hear Him whisper—
Create. Be my poetry.
Find your voice. Offer something honest.
Feel my peace and joy rest in you.
Shine brilliantly. You are My Work of Art.

"We are God's work of art.
He has created us anew in Christ Jesus."

EPHESIANS 2:10

"Why give a flower fragrance? Could it be God loves to see the look on your face? You aren't an accident or an incident. You are a gift to the world, a divine work of art, signed by God." MAX LUCADO

I woke up to the sound of autumn's first rain, after a long draught in a sun-scorched California summer.

So I put on my shoes, took my raincoat and umbrella, drove to a nearby trail, and walked across a wooden bridge dotted with freshly fallen wet leaves. It was so quiet and peaceful, I whispered, "Thank you, God." I was thanking Him for the rain. Yet He sees deeper.

God's been listening to all my unspoken whispers—in the places my soul has been dry, needing to be filled. And I felt Him whisper in return: *You don't have to wonder... I am making all things new again. Like poetry, you were meant to reflect beauty.*

Think of everything that is beautiful. Then remember that everything beautiful was meant to be made new in you. With God. Together.

> *"Then I will send rain on your land in its season,*
> *both autumn and spring rains,*
> *so that you may gather in your grain, new wine and*
> *olive oil."* DEUTERONOMY 11:14

There is new grain. New wine. New oil. For you. In you.

Artwork. Poetry. Could this be the new wine and new oil God wants you to receive so you can shine as the Beloved for Him? You were never created to simply survive, only to be useful and functional, like a robot on autopilot.

God invites you into a new season—to follow Him as His Beloved and create, instead of living like a slave, constantly toiling to produce.

God asks you to creatively express your feelings, your story, and who you are—through art. *Your Heavenly Father loves to see you shine and be creative just like Him.* Be an artist, shining His light of beauty into the world.

Get in touch with the *artistic you.* Express your creativity. *Let go of controlling what happens after you create.* People may or may not like it. We have to let go of our time lines and our need to measure how good our art is.

To create something beautiful as the Beloved, we need to simply be honest.

You Are God's Work of Art

Create. Lay aside all your fears and bare your heart with Jesus on the canvas—through your brush, the words you write, the movements you dance, the notes you play, or the voice you echo through photography, needle, thread, clay, yarn, pen, paper, or stylus.

Like soft autumn leaves turning crimson-gold, hear God's gentle voice invite you to create space to allow Him to express His artwork in you. *Being creative is a journey of finding your voice.* Creativity is a discovery of faith that heals the soul, because you don't know how it will unfold. You just have to let go and see where it leads.

Let go of what is and has been, so God can bring new grain, new wine, and new oil to reignite your heart again.

Be God's work of art. Find your voice.

READ GOD'S STORY

Stop and breathe. Notice whatever is beautiful around you that God created to inspire you today. Look at the leaves rustling in the breeze on the tree, the smile in your daughter's eyes, the sound your guitar makes, the curve of your boyfriend's chin, or the sunlight resting on your hand. See the beauty around you.

Listen to God whisper—*Be still. Let me shine through you.*

"Be still and know that I am God." PSALM 46:10

Being still and listening engages you in doing something creative. Nothing else exists in that moment, except what you and God are both experiencing together.

God has imprinted the longing to create in everyone. Just give yourself the chance to be curious. Then, follow that quiet desire by faith with Jesus. Reflect on this truth—

"For we are God's masterpiece—his work of art.
He has created us anew in Christ Jesus."
EPHESIANS 2:10

The original Greek word, which translates as "work of art" or "masterpiece," is *poeima*—from which we get our English word "poetry."

Assure your heart. You *are* God's work of art. Nothing else matters. *You are His poetry.* All is well.

✒ *God's Whispers to You*

Beloved,
Just as the leaves turn crimson-gold in autumn,

falling to reflect the touch of my finger,
fall into my creative embrace today.

Create. Be my poetry.
Find your voice. Offer something honest.
Feel my peace and joy rest in you.
Shine brilliantly. You are my Work of Art.

✐ A Prayer for Today: Create and Shine as God's Work of Art

"We are God's work of art.
He has created us anew in Christ Jesus."

EPHESIANS 2:10

Dear Jesus,
Thank you for making me like you,
with a desire to create.
Open my eyes to see
the beautiful things you want me to make.

Give me inspiration and courage to shine your light.
Help me to have fun and enjoy
doing something creative with you today.
Fill me with your peace and joy,
as I follow my curiosity and find my voice with you.
Amen.

Sometimes, the world can be such a noisy place—always calling for us to be stronger, to move faster—to hurt less and always know the answers.

Yet, the leaves of autumn tell us a secret. *The hush of rain tip-tapping on the ground reminds us of the beautiful poetry and art-work He's planted deep in you.*

Shining with Jesus by creating may be new for you. It's okay. Like the flutters of a butterfly's wings breaking from its cocoon, Jesus assures us: *I am making all things new in you. I will create with you.* Create and be God's Beloved today.

Give Yourself Permission: What's beauty to you? See, hear, taste, make, and smell. Create. Buy some supplies. Take a class. You don't have to be good at it. All you need is curiosity.

REFLECT ON YOUR STORY

1. *How is God stirring curiosity in you—to enjoy doing something creative or explore and try something new?*

2. *What form of the creative arts are you drawn to?*
   —*Visual arts: painting, drawing, ceramics*
   —*Performing arts: music, dance, theatre*
   —*Literary arts: poetry, novels, short stories*
   —*Culinary arts: baking, cooking*
   —*Media arts: photography, cinematography*

3. *What One Word speaks to you today?*

PRAY & REST

A SIMPLE PRACTICE: POETRY AS PRAYER

Flannery O'Connor prayed by writing poetry in *A Prayer Journal*:

> *Dear God, I cannot love Thee the way I want to.*
> *You are the slim crescent of a moon that I see*
> *and my self is the earth's shadow*
> *that keeps me from seeing all the moon . . .*
> *I do not mean to deny the traditional prayers . . .*
> *but I have been saying them and not feeling them . . . This way,*
> *I have it every instant. I can feel a warmth of love heating me*
> *when I think & write this to You.*

Today, write a poem, inspired by your One Word pick. Let it be your prayer.

—— *∅ ∅ ∅* ——

TODAY'S BELOVED CHALLENGE

Do Something Artistic
Create art. Read poetry. View artwork.
Schedule a visit to a gallery.

Let the whispers of thanksgiving no longer be the words you say, but a *prayer that you live*—through the art you create with Jesus today.

SOUL CARE TRAIL NOTES

Create Art and Feel Happier and Healthier

Express your God-given creativity and feel happier and healthier. A wealth of studies show that simple, creative hobbies like crafting—knitting, quilting, sewing, gardening (anything do-it-yourself)—or coloring, painting, drawing, and photography provide wonderful benefits:

- *Creating Art Relieves Stress.* Creating puts you in a meditative state called "flow," restoring mental clarity and calm.
- *Art Increases Resilience and Creativity, and Helps Prevent Memory Loss,* enhancing brain plasticity.
- *Simply Viewing Art Triggers Happy Hormones* in the brain. Brain scans revealed that looking at artwork triggers a surge of dopamine in the areas of the brain that register romantic love.

Story

Illuminate My Love. You Are My Story.

The world doesn't need perfect people.
The world needs shelter. To be loved.
We all long to be perfectly loved.

Jesus whispers,
Be real.
Illuminate my love
by sharing your story.
You are my Story.

"You are a letter of Christ, cared for by us,
written not with ink, but with the Spirit of the living God,
not on tablets of stone but on tablets of human hearts."

2 CORINTHIANS 3:3

"After nourishment, shelter and companionship, stories are the thing we need most in the world."

PHILIP PULLMAN

I've tried to write for everyone else. Except for me. I'm not talking about the book. I'm talking about my life.

I couldn't find my voice. Even though it seemed to always come alive whenever I wrote in my journal as a little girl, I stopped journaling after college. I wrote papers as a college student and, later for work, as a high-tech professional. But I forgot about words. The ones from my heart. I didn't think it was important to talk about what was happening and how I felt. *What would be the point?* I told myself.

The best way I thought to love God was to stay faithful to do things for him and put away whatever discouraged me and focus on serving others. I loved people.

But I was quiet about the chapters in my story that wounded me. I incorrectly believed that shining for God meant cutting out the parts of my life that felt broken or "unshiny." I didn't want to be different. I wanted to belong.

But that light in me that once sparkled in the night as I poured my heart out to God as a little girl began to dim. It began to dim because God doesn't speak through a disconnected heart. I was so good at editing my story to make it safe and acceptable, I lost the ability to feel honestly and express my soul to God. By losing touch with the moments that brought me loneliness and pain, I also extinguished the ones that sparked joy, passion, and hope.

Whenever we hide, shame like walls of stone will separate us from the childlike spirit and curiosity God uniquely created in you and me. It is in the intimate spaces of your story that God speaks and shines His light of love and faithfulness—through every event, conversation, and emotion He experienced with you, as it inspired or broke you.

Your heart—*your whole story*—is the living temple where the Holy Spirit breathes and speaks to others through your voice and mine (see 1 Corinthians 3:16).

God speaks through real people who are living real stories.

God is an Artist and He takes every part of your story—your hopes and dreams, but also your tears and doubts—to make faith beautiful and real. *You are God's living story.*

It's true. Jesus once invited his disciples who were hiding behind closed doors after he died to say—*Come closer. See the scars on my hands and my side. I'm real.*

His wounds didn't disappear with his resurrected body. *Jesus chose to walk out into the world with his scars from the past—visible.* With those hands he reaches out to gently invite you to welcome others to him through your story. The Holy Spirit lives in *every part of you* today. As is.

What is the story that God wants to illuminate in you to show His love to others through you?

The Gift of Your Story

Living in a digital world where our online identities are crafted by the words and images we post, we have the power to share what we think people will like and hide the rest. Image crafting works well to build a following or sell a product. But it isn't real.

We were created to share something more beautiful with each other. *You were created to shine a spotlight on God's story in you.* The parts of me I usually like to hide are the very parts where God is working in my life and my story. Could this be true for your story, too?

The world doesn't need any more cookie-cutter stories that hide the realities of life and keep us emotionally distant from each other because we're afraid of appearing odd or broken. The truth is that everyone has a story. The world doesn't need any more perfect people. *What the world needs is shelter.* Life is imperfect. We all long to be perfectly loved.

We need the gift of shelter and kindness in this demanding world that pushes us to be busy and perfect. So share your story, and you'll show something living and beautiful that is uniquely yours from God. You will welcome others to be loved and find respite—and share their stories, too.

"Stories are verbal acts of hospitality."

EUGENE PETERSON

Your story offers the gift of shelter. Be real. Your story has the power to give us courage when we feel weak, to inspire us to write new chapters—inviting us to share our stories with a kindred spirit who understands.

God wants to use you. *Will you let God write a new chapter— or even a new story—in you today?*

READ GOD'S STORY

We are God's living story, but we often like to fill in the blanks and avoid uncertainty. Hear God's radical encouragement to you through the angel Gabriel's words to Mary—

"Nothing, you see, is impossible with God."   LUKE 1:37

Do we actually believe that God can do *anything*? Mary could have responded—

"Not now . . ."

"Not me..."
"Not this way..."
"But..."
Instead, Mary believed:

"Yes, I see it all now:
I'm the Lord's...
Let it be with me just as you say."   LUKE 1:37-38

It dawned on me. *What Mary saw* wasn't *how* things would work out. Mary had no idea what was ahead, but she was willing to trust. To believe she was beloved.

What Mary did see was that *God would fill in the blanks.* *She was willing to be that space* for His story.

Today, God extends the same invitation to us. *Illuminate God's love through your story.* Let God write His story in you.

✏ *God's Whispers to You*

Beloved,
It is time for you to shine.
I don't want you just when you are strong.
I love you even when you feel broken.
And I don't find it shameful when you are real.

You want to speak only in a voice that feels safe and good.
But I want you to speak in your whole voice,
where I am your only safety, where I am your only good.

Nothing is impossible for me.
Be real. Illuminate my love through your story.
Let me write my story in you.

If you're feeling overwhelmed by chapters that appear barren, remember Jesus is faithful to bring *beautiful things to life in you. Your story is the portrait in which God's light of love shines.* And if you wonder if anything beautiful shines in you, asking *How can this be?*—remember Jesus is weaving an epic love story in you.

✐ *A Prayer for Today*:
Illuminate God's Story in You

"I'm the Lord's…
Let it be with me just as you say."   LUKE 1:38

Dear Jesus,
Give me courage to take a leap of faith,
To be the space for your story
And write new chapters with you.

Give me courage to speak in my whole voice.
To shine a spotlight on your love in every part of me.
Let it be with me. Just as you say.
For nothing is impossible for you, God.

Kindle your spark in me again.
Thank you for loving and choosing me.
I want to be your story. Shine in me today.
Amen.

Faith is as mysterious as it is real. Faith is a living journey. It finds a way.

I'm beginning to understand. A word—your story—even if small as a mustard seed will grow to become a beautiful tree offering shelter and rest in its branches. Jesus is quietly writing the most beautiful stories of faith where your heart is tender, virgin, and untouched.

> *"Let us throw off every encumbrance…*
> *fixing our eyes on Jesus, the author and perfecter*
> *of our faith."*   HEBREWS 12:1–2

One day, you'll see the entire story that Jesus is authoring and perfecting in you, when we see him face-to-face. Until then, God has given you a voice and a blank page called life to write those stories—by living them out in your everyday joys, sorrows, dreams, and even loss. It's *all* beautiful in God's eyes, because it is *real*.

Be God's living story. Let's share the stories we're living as kindred on this journey of faith. It's not always easy. But sometimes the harder stories are the ones worth telling.

Give Yourself Permission: Write a new chapter. Illuminate God's love in your story. Be real.

REFLECT ON YOUR STORY

1. *How can you take a leap of faith and be the space for God's story?*

2. *What are the parts of your story God doesn't want you to hide but share to illuminate His love to others?*

3. *What kind of books do you enjoy getting lost in?*

4. *What One Word speaks to you today?*

PRAY & REST

A SIMPLE PRACTICE: LET IT BE WITH ME AS YOU SAY

Our prayer today is inspired by Mary's prayer to be space for God's story. Pastor and scholar Eugene Peterson, who wrote *The Message*, powerfully reminds us, "Stories are verbal acts of hospitality."

Today's One Word Prayer is *STORY*. Will you allow your story to welcome others into God's refuge, kindness, and kinship? Then you must open your heart to invite Jesus into your most honest moments of joy, sorrow, and desire—where faith becomes your ink and your voice its pen.

Prayer is the intimate movement to write a story of love with God.

Jesus, this is the new story you're birthing in me . . .

This is the leap of faith I want to take . . .

Close this time by praying—*Let it be with me as you say . . .*

TODAY'S BELOVED CHALLENGE

Read a Printed Book
Turn some actual pages.
Put away electronic devices and breathe.

"Books are the quietest and most constant of friends"
(Charles W. Eliot). Rest and refresh your soul.

Read Your Way to Tranquility and Good Sleep

SOUL CARE TRAIL NOTES

Reading is the best way to relax, and even six minutes can be enough to reduce stress levels by more than two-thirds, according to research carried out at Sussex University. Snuggling up with a good book returns rest and tranquility to your brain and body, as you get lost in a story and unplug from constantly multitasking during the day (which is exhausting).

Reading helps you destress faster than listening to music, taking a walk, or having a cup of tea or coffee, according to the study. When researchers measured heart rate and muscle tension, people relaxed six minutes into reading.

The Mayo Clinic also found that reading a book for twenty minutes as a bedtime ritual helps signal your body to sleep. Read a print book. It helps you relax more than reading on your tablet or watching a show, because looking at screens actually keeps you awake longer and hurts your sleep.

DAY 39

Song

Shine bright and new. You are my Song.

Come, thou fount of every blessing,
Tune my heart to sing thy grace;
Streams of mercy, never ceasing,
Call for songs of loudest praise.
Teach me some melodious sonnet,
Sung by flaming tongues above.
Praise the mount! I'm fixed upon it,
Mount of thy redeeming love.

ROBERT ROBINSON,
"COME THOU FOUNT OF EVERY BLESSING," 1757

"By day the Lord directs his love, at night his song is with me—a prayer to the God of my life."

PSALM 42:8

"He has given me a new song to sing."   PSALM 40:3

"Music can change the world because it can change people." BONO

I remember the first time I heard it sing. I sat there transfixed by the sound, six years tall, having never seen the inside of a church before. The notes filled the room like flowers in bloom, as the sunlight fell from the window across the hardwood floor to come to rest at my feet. I had never been so close to a live instrument, but I could feel the music hum through my chest.

It was the voice of the piano. I could see the back post of the upright, exposing her ribs, supporting the soundboard, as rich four-note chords of a hymn brightly lit up the room. I don't remember the words from the sermon that day. But I will never forget how I felt that morning and every Sunday when the piano played.

I felt God's peace. I felt His comfort and His arms lifting me in joy before I recognized it was His voice. I began to find that whenever I felt lonely, walking home from school or as I lay awake at night—whenever I needed His touch—a song would come to my heart.

God whispered to me through song before I ever understood it was His presence. Music was God's light in my life, and it moved me to feel what I could not express.

Today God continues to sing of His love and peace to the world through you. *God shines His light in the dark places because you are His song.*

You Are God's Song

Sometimes, we may wonder how we can leave our mark in this world. Jesus tells us we are his light, but we can't see how our ordinary, everyday self has anything unique to offer. It is easy to feel an unrest that can grow frantic, as we search for our calling. It is tempting to view our lives as insignificant until we somehow find our calling—*in something that we do.*

But as we see from those who experienced God most intimately—like Elijah who while running away, heard God in a still hush instead of an earthquake or a fire, like Moses, who felt God's hand cover him as he hid behind a rock, or like Mary Magdalene, who recognized Jesus only after he whispered her name as she wept—*we find our greatest calling in who we become as God's Beloved.* We move to the tune of God's love.

> "For the love of Christ compels us."
>
> 2 CORINTHIANS 5:14

> "See how very much our Father loves us, for he calls us his children."
>
> 1 JOHN 3:1

Like a song, you are shining God's light through sharing the simple things that bring you peace, joy, and comfort. You bring music to the broken places that only God can mend. When you share your gift, your story, your art—to reveal pain or beauty—with your friends, family, coworkers, and even strangers, something honest and real is given. Without preaching a word, *you become the Gospel.*

The more you are able to rest in who God made you to be, the more others will experience God's presence through you. By simply being you, you'll sing God's song of kindness and friendship as you laugh, cry, listen, or offer a smile with your hello. You are free to be God's song right where you are. As is.

▚ READ GOD'S STORY ▚

Quiet your heart now. Let the songs that the Psalmist David penned from his soul become seed for your prayer. Notice the word or phrase that speaks to you as you read the verses below. Reflect on how God is your song today.

> *"When I remember you on my bed,*
> *I meditate on you in the night watches.*
>
> *For you have been my help,*
> *and in the shadow of your wings I sing for joy."*
>
> PSALM 63:6–7

> *"You are my hiding place;*
> *you will protect me from trouble*
> *and surround me with songs of deliverance."*
>
> PSALM 32:7

> *"He put a new song in my mouth, a song of praise."*
>
> PSALM 40:3

> *"Sing praise to the Lord,*
> *And give thanks to His holy name…*
> *Weeping may last through the night,*
> *but joy comes with the morning."*   PSALM 30:4–5

> *"But let all who take refuge in you be glad,*
> *Let them ever sing for joy;*
> *And may you shelter them."*   PSALM 5:11

Listen again. Hear His whispers for you.

☞ *God's Whispers to You*

Beloved,
In the darkness, where this world longs to be held and known,
I am lighting the way home back to me through you.

Whether in major or minor key,
I am singing my love song in the night,
to bring comfort, peace, and joy through your voice.

Let me have my way in you.
Shine bright. Sing new. You are my Song.
You are my Beloved.

For our prayer today, I want to share the lyrics to a song that my friend Ryan Kingsmith wrote, "Weakness Redefined." This song became a prayer that lit my journey through many nights, leading to the whispers of rest held in your hands today.

☞ *A Prayer for Today*: Sing a New Song

"By day the Lord directs his love, at night his song is with me—a prayer to the God of my life."   PSALM 42:8

"He has given me a new song to sing."   PSALM 40:3

Dear Jesus,
Lord of all the earth and the universe,

I'll sing you a prayer, may my words be yours
God of love and God of hope.

The ballad of my failure is a mile long
Change the tune and make me sing a brand-new song
Write a lovely melody . . .

You're as beautiful as music from a violin
Break all of the bonds I've constructed
Then draw me to yourself
Make me more like you
Then and only then will I be made new.
Amen.

We no longer have to be desperate to find our calling. There is Someone who died a thousand times over so he can sing his song in you, through your dreams and even through your deepest pain. Your voice is significant because Jesus is in you.

Be bold. Keep being brave. Sing your song, kindred. You are beloved.

Give Yourself Permission: Rest in your greatest calling— who you are as God's Beloved. Like a song, shine God's light through sharing the simple things that bring you peace, joy, and comfort. Others will experience God's presence through you. Without preaching a word, *you become the Gospel.* Sing a new song.

REFLECT ON YOUR STORY

1. *What can you do today to renew your spirit with peace, joy and comfort?*

2. *What kind of music do you enjoy? How does music enrich your life?*

3. *How can you sing a new song today?*

4. *What One Word speaks to you in today's Scripture?*

PRAY & REST

A SIMPLE PRACTICE: WORSHIP WITH MUSIC

Fanny Crosby, born blind, was the amazing writer of "Blessed Assurance" and over eight thousand other hymns. She said, "It is not enough to have a song on your lips. You must have a song on your heart."

Today's One Word Prayer is *SONG*. *What song is God singing in your heart?* Listen to it on repeat three times, as a way to be present with God. Sit, lie down, or kneel. Allow the Holy Spirit to touch you. Let the song guide you to rest. If you play an instrument, experience His presence that way. Linger in the moment.

Jesus, I love this song _____. It reflects my heart's prayer because . . .

TODAY'S BELOVED CHALLENGE

What Is Your Special Song?
Listen to the music. Sing. Relish the lyrics.
Rejuvenate your soul.

You are God's song. Shine bright.

SOUL CARE TRAIL NOTES

Rejuvenate Your Soul with the Power of a Song

A song's ability to rejuvenate emotional connection is real. Songs powerfully reconnect us to our most important emotional experiences—by sparking memories of significant experiences with people we love and the life-changing events, challenges or transitions we undergo, along with the feelings, sights, or sounds that impacted us most deeply. That's because the region of the brain where memories are stored serves as a hub that links music to memories and emotion.

It's also why people suffering memory loss due to Alzheimer's disease perk up when they hear a song from their past. They brighten up, express emotion, sing along, and even dance. Music therapy not only destresses, calms anxieties, and improves sleep, but it allows us to reexperience a loved one's presence. A song triggers the sound of their voice, and we relive the emotional memories of intimacy, peace, and joy.

DAY 40

✿ ✿ ✿

Treasure

You were made to shine. You are my Treasure.

The Voice of Love calls to you,
like a song in the night—
Like a diamond in the sky,
you were made to shine.

I have given up everything
to love you back to life again.
You are my pearl of great value.
You are my Treasure.

"For God who said, "Let light shine out of darkness,"
made His light shine in our hearts…in the face of Jesus
Christ.

"Now we have this treasure in jars of clay to show that
this surpassing great power is from God and not
from us."   2 CORINTHIANS 4:6–7

"We can only be said to be alive in those moments when our hearts are conscious of our treasures."

THORNTON WILDER

I love autumn. It's a quiet time, when the leaves fall from branch to earth, changing colors as the breeze gently carries them to rest at our feet. I love hearing the crunch of foliage after it settles like a blanket on the trail and the mornings return to a cool crisp.

Later, when the rain falls, dry creek beds soon glimmer with moving water, catching sunlight, trickling leaves over rocks, like petals floating in the sky.

What was your favorite season as a little girl? What memories do you treasure most?

Maybe it isn't autumn, but the stillness of winter's bare trees. As snow silently descends at night and sparkles to say hello in the morning, you love to snuggle in your favorite sweater, make hot chocolate, and reach for a book by a warm fire.

Maybe it's springtime you love best. You feel happy as flowers bloom, birds sing at your window, and the smell of fresh rain returns a song to your heart.

Then there is summer, which brings the joy of sand castles, road trips, and running through sprinklers. Do you savor the sunny months best, when you could ride your bike, free of backpacks and schoolwork, or plop down on the sofa with a melting orange popsicle in your hand?

You Are God's Treasure

In all these memories, look back again now and see the One who has always been with you, watching you enjoy each moment and speaking joy, peace or comfort to you. Can you see? You are God's Treasure.

See Jesus painting each sunset you've ever seen dip into twilight in the sky so you could experience the beauty in his heart as he experienced each memory with you. In every season of your life, Jesus has been loving you, whispering words of rest.

Jesus has been walking with you, even to this very place where your forty-day devotional journey ends today.

Picture yourself now standing at the edge of a beach, the water softly lapping at your feet. Look across the horizon and see a boat drifting in place among the waves. The dawn is just beginning to break, and you can still see the last stars of the night, lingering to hold their place.

There, close by, you see a man sitting on the shore and kindling a fire. You watch him slowly rise and step in the direction of the boat. As your eyes adjust to morning's first light, you realize he is someone you know.

You recognize him. It's Jesus.

READ GOD'S STORY

Jesus is standing at the Sea of Galilee—and that boat you see? It's the disciples'. Jesus died, so they've gone back to what's familiar, back to what they were used to doing, before Jesus called them to follow him. They fished the whole night. But they caught nothing.

As you stand at the end of this forty-day journey, God has been rejuvenating your soul with His whispers of rest. You may also be asking yourself, "What will this new season bring? Has life really changed or will life return to the familiar?"

Listen now and be present with Jesus in this final scene where Jesus spent his last hours with his closest friends, before he had to leave and ascend to heaven. Of all the people in power he could have appeared to, to prove he was alive, Jesus chose instead to quietly love his disciples one-on-one.

Jesus wants to love you right now in the same way. Read this passage from John 21:4–13 *slowly*. Place yourself next to Jesus as this story unfolds, as if it were happening with you there today.

At dawn, Jesus was standing on the beach, but the disciples couldn't see who he was. He called out to them, "Friends, haven't you any fish?"

"No," they answered.

He said, "Throw your net on the right side of the boat and you will find some." When they did, they were unable to haul the net in because of the large number of fish.

Then the disciple whom Jesus loved said to Peter, "It is the Lord!" As soon as Simon Peter heard him say, "It is the Lord," he wrapped his outer garment around him and jumped into the water.

The other disciples followed in the boat, towing the net full of fish. When they landed, they saw a fire of burning coals there with fish on it, and some bread.

Jesus said to them, "Bring some of the fish you have just caught."

So Simon Peter climbed back into the boat and dragged the net ashore. It was full of large fish, 153, but even with so many, the net was not torn.

Jesus said to them, "Come and have breakfast."

Jesus came, took the bread and gave it to them, and did the same with the fish.

Read the passage a second time now. Notice the One Word or phrase that draws your attention—that touches you most deeply.

How do you feel as you see Jesus making breakfast for you? How do you feel as He speaks to you?

His One Word for You

See Jesus look into your eyes. See the kindness and his quiet understanding. He knows how tired you are, toiling all night. He loves you.

Hear him whisper, *Come and have breakfast.* Feel his hand guiding you to sit next to him. Watch Jesus slowly turn the fish over the fire, until the skin tightens slightly, because it means the flesh has grown tender and sweet underneath. It is ready for you to eat.

Jesus could have turned stones to bread. Easily. Instead, Jesus places the bread next to the fish over a fire, so it will slowly soften and warm you, as he places it into your hands.

Now picture the One Word that spoke to you as you read the passage. See Jesus place this One Word in your hand. This is your bread. His holy presence. Manna. *His whispers of rest coming alive in your soul today.* It will give you strength for the journey. Taste how sweet it is.

"I am the living bread that came down from heaven.

Whoever eats this bread will live forever."   JOHN 6:51

You have everything you need for this journey ahead. You

have Jesus, the One who loves you. He will never leave you as an orphan, but calls you Beloved today and forever.

✒ *God's Whispers to You*

Beloved,
I am always with you.
I always have been,
and I'll never leave you.

You are my very treasure.
My very pearl, for whom I have given up everything,
to call you my very own.

Nothing can ever separate me from loving you.
No trouble, no hardship,
No persecution, no hunger,
No danger or even death itself,
can tear me away from you.

I will never be parted from you.
You are my very heart.
You are my very home.

For I bore forty lashes until it broke and bled my body,
dying as I thought of you in my last breath.
I was raised back to life to love you faithfully.
Unconditionally. Never-ending.

Beloved, I am right here interceding for you—
praying day and night with you and for you.

One day, you and I will be reunited. Forever.
And there will be no more night.
Because I will be your moon and your stars.
I will be your everything.
I am your Beloved and you are mine.

Until then,
Shine. You are my Beloved.
Shine. You are mine forever.
Shine. You are my Treasure.

✑ A Prayer for Today: Shine Radiantly—You Are God's Treasure

For God who said, "Let light shine out of darkness," made His light shine in our hearts…in the face of Jesus Christ.

Now we have this treasure in jars of clay to show that this surpassing great power is from God and not from us. 2 CORINTHIANS 4:6–7

Dear Jesus,
You are my Treasure.
You are my Greatest Reward.
All that entangles me, I give now to you.
Break the bonds so I can run free in your love—to you.

Build a fire so bright within me for you.
Empower me with your Holy Spirit,
To move as you move.

To stop and pray each day.
To love you as my First Love,
Without regard for anything, other than to bring you pleasure.
Rejuvenate my soul with your Word
and bless me to live with you and for you.

Thank you for the manna you have given me these forty days.
Thank you for hearing me when I pray,
For being the Living Bread in me.
Thank you for your Holy Presence,
Loving me so tenderly and unequivocally,
intimately and fully.
Thank you for your Whispers of Rest for me.

I love you.
You are beautiful.
You are my Beloved.
Forever.
Amen.

Sweet kindred, do you wonder if all this beauty—of who you really are to Jesus—is really true for you? Listen. Jesus answers you:

Then the righteous will shine like the sun
in the kingdom of their Father...

*The kingdom of heaven is **like a treasure***
that a man discovered hidden in a field.
In his excitement, he hid it again, and sold everything
he owned to get enough money to buy the field.

*Again, the kingdom of heaven is like a merchant in
search of fine pearls.*
*When he discovered **a pearl of great value**,*
he sold everything he owned and bought it.

MATTHEW 13:43–46

It *is* all true of you. Every whisper. Every promise is God's
yes to you.

You are His Beloved. Today and always.

Give Yourself Permission: Shine. You are God's forever. You are His Greatest Treasure. Shine. Shine. Shine.

REFLECT ON YOUR STORY

1. *What is the One Word Jesus placed in your hand today—the Living Word that he spoke in today's Scriptures? What is Jesus saying to you?*

2. *Now write your prayer in response to Jesus. Capture all that is flowing from his heart to yours and from yours to his.*

PRAY & REST

A SIMPLE PRACTICE: GRATITUDE

"To be grateful is to recognize the Love of God in everything He has given us—and He has given us everything. Every breath we draw is a gift of His love, every moment of existence is grace."
THOMAS MERTON

Now it's your turn.

Dear Jesus, my Forever Beloved, thank you for all I've received these forty days . . .

TODAY'S BELOVED CHALLENGE

Start a Gratitude Journal
List three things you are thankful for.
How are you experiencing God's love, peace, or joy?

Hear God whisper, "Shine like a diamond. You are my Treasure."

SOUL CARE TRAIL NOTES

Transform and Revitalize Your Soul with Gratitude

A wealth of scientific studies prove that cultivating gratitude by noticing positive experiences—even in the midst of stress and turmoil—combined with expressing thankfulness transforms our emotional and our physical health. Powerful benefits include:

- Reducing stress, anxiety, depression, and headaches
- Decreasing blood pressure, and strengthening the immune system and heart health
- Greater happiness, joy, and optimism
- Less loneliness, more social, compassionate, and forgiving
- Increasing vitality, energy, and enlivening emotions

Research shows that *two weeks* of keeping a gratitude journal to write down daily experiences you're thankful for have positive effects that *last up to six months*.

҂ ҂ ҂

Parting Whispers

"I have loved you with an everlasting love;
I have drawn you with unfailing kindness."

JEREMIAH 31:3

I've wondered, could the girl with stars in her eyes ever come back to me?

As we come to the end of our forty-day journey, I am thankful that we've shared this journey of returning to our First Love. We've found our spark again with God's whispers of rest, revitalizing our soul with His love in new ways.

Now we no longer have to wonder if the girl with stars in her eyes would return—because she is right here, shining brightly as God's Beloved. She is in you and in me. Take good care of her. Remind her how important she is to God. Nurture her spirit. Listen to her heart. Confide always in Jesus, the One who holds the hand of the child in you and enfolds you close into his embrace.

You are God's Beloved. And so am I.

Sparkle Again

As I wrote each line in this guidebook, I prayed that you would experience Jesus intimately and be revitalized with God's love to dare, dream, and shine as His Beloved. My hope is that you are now holding the most beautiful treasure in your hands: a journal of the most intimate prayers and conversations between you and Jesus uncovered during these forty days.

And for those of you who invited friends to share the journey and read this book together, I hope that you've found a deeper kinship because of the stories you've shared, that you are better known and refreshed by the encouragement of friends.

As I've shared my heart and my stories as a fellow kindred, I want to thank you for the gift of your stories, the grace of your time, and your presence between these pages. We no longer have to journey alone. I'm grateful for you.

I can't wait to meet you one day and hear all about the beautiful ways God's whispers of rest have refreshed your soul with His love. *Continue to let God love you, and I'll be thinking of you whenever I look at the stars and find them twinkling with beauty in the night sky.*

Share your story. Share your art. Share your voice. Share your song.

Sparkle again. Shine brightly. You are beautiful.

Remember: You're loved. You're cherished. You're worth it. *You are the Beloved. Just rest.*

Acknowledgments

The journey to write *Whispers of Rest* began with a seed of an idea. Early on, you only show that seed to someone who loves you more than the idea, because you don't know if it's meant to grow, lay dormant or die that very day. Eric, you are that one, special person who has seen my dreams conceived, with many drifting away like a dandelion puff, while only some succeed. You've grieved and celebrated with me in joy and sorrow. Eric, thank you for having the courage to dream with me again, for lovingly encouraging me, and praying for this book to blossom. I love you.

Thank you to my loving sons Josh and Caleb who encourage and pray for me, celebrating with frozen yogurt and dubbing this book "Mommy's passion project."

Writing from the soul is vulnerable, daunting work. You become exposed to whether others will deem your voice worthy. So, here I must thank my agent and friend, Chip Mac-Gregor, a kindred spirit who always tells me, "Write it the way you want, Bonnie." And helps me navigate the publishing waters so expertly.

Thank you to my amazing publishing team at Hachette FaithWords for tirelessly investing heart, energy and vision — delivering the highest quality book I'm so proud of. Special gratitude goes to my senior editor Keren Baltzer, marketing director Andrea Glickson, online marketing manager Katie O'Connor, editor Virginia Bhashkar, and publicist Sarah Falter. God's best gifts in you shines through this release.

And when the apostle Paul felt afraid, because people rejected him in Corinth, Jesus appeared to him one night and said, "Don't be afraid. Keep speaking...For I am with you, and no one is...going to harm you, because I have many people in this city." And so with deep gratitude, I say *thank you* to my readers and the friends I've met as I traveled to speak – for your stories and your loving support for me as an author.

Without you, kindred readers, this book would not be here. *You are my people – The people God put in cities where you live. Where you welcome me into your heart and on your journey. You make me brave.* You are God's treasure.

Thank you to my in-real-life friends who encourage me, who drank a ridiculous amount of tea or coffee, as I wrestled with the writing: Sally Forster, Carol Hursh, Merrianne Young, Michelle Dunn, Rose Negrete, Elaine Herbert, Juanita Li, Grace Kvamme, Pastor John Riemenschnitter, Kevin Marks, Coach Ken Mburu and Dr. John Patterson, along with many more. A special thank you goes to gifted Micayla Brewster, who gave this book social media wings.

And to the One who is my beginning and who will love me to the very end – *Jesus.* Thank you for never abandoning me, always whispering words of rest with your never-ending-always-faithful love. Thank you for renaming me *Beloved.* Keep holding me close to you. You are mine. And I am yours.

Book Resources

Foster, Richard. *Prayer: Finding the Heart's True Home*. HarperOne, 2002.
————, and James Smith, eds. *Devotional Classics: Selected Readings for Individuals and Groups*. HarperSanFrancisco, 1993.

Book References of Author Quotes featured in "Pray & Rest" or "Today's Beloved Challenge" section

Day 1: Keller, Timothy. *Prayer: Experiencing Awe and Intimacy with God*. Viking, 2014.

Day 2: Lucado, Max. http://www.christiantoday.com/article/max.lucado.too.many.christians.think.god.isnt.listening.to.their.prayers.because.they.did.not.pray.correctly/47450.htm.

Day 3: Warren, Rick. https://twitter.com/rickwarren/status/620711129036165120.

Day 4: Teresa of Avila. *The Interior Castle*. Riverhead Books, 2004.

Day 5: Brother Lawrence. *The Practice of the Presence of God*. Translated by John J. Delaney. Doubleday, 1977.

Day 6: Kierkegaard, Søren. *Purity of the Heart Is to Will One Thing*. Harper & Brothers, 1938.

Day 7: Baillie, John. *A Diary of a Private Prayer*. 0Scribner, 2014.

Day 8: Nouwen, Henri. *Here and Now: Living in the Spirit*. Crossroad Publishing, 2006.

Day 9: Foster, Richard. *The Celebration of Discipline: The Path to Spiritual Growth*. HarperSanFrancisco, 1998.

Day 10: Swenson, Richard. *The Overload Syndrome*. NavPress, 1999.

Day 11: Luther, Martin. *Table Talk*. Beloved Publishing, 2014.

Day 12: Peterson, Eugene. *The Jesus Way: Conversations on the Ways That Jesus Is the Way*. Eerdmans, 2011.

Bonhoeffer, Dietrich. *Life Together.* HarperOne, 2009.

Day 13: L'Engle, Madeleine. *A Circle of Quiet.* HarperOne, 1984.

Day 14: Stedman, Ray. *How to Live What You Believe.* Regal Books, 1974.

Day 15: Barton, Ruth Haley. *Invitation to Solitude and Silence: Experience God's Transforming Presence.* IVP Books, 2010.

Day 16: Guyon, Jeanne. *Experiencing the Depths of Jesus Christ.* Christian Books, 1981.

Day 17: Spurgeon, Charles. "Charles Spurgeon." In *Devotional Classics: Selected Readings for Individuals and Groups,* edited by Richard Foster and James Smith. HarperSanFrancisco, 1993, p. 333.

Day 18: Ortberg, John. "Getting Good at Prayer Isn't the Point." *Christianity Today,* Summer 2015. http://www.christianitytoday.com/le/2015/summer-2015/getting-good-at-prayer-isnt-point.html?start=4.

———. *Soul Keeping.* Zondervan, 2014.

Day 19: Foster, Richard. *Prayer: Finding the Heart's True Home.* HarperOne, 2002.

Day 20: Guyon, Jeanne. *Experiencing the Depths of Jesus Christ*; Foster, Richard, *Prayer: Finding the Heart's True Home.*

Day 21: ten Boom, Corrie. *The Hiding Place.* Chosen Books, 2006.

Day 23: Francis of Assisi. *The Little Flowers of Saint Francis,* translated by Thomas Okey. Dover, 2003.

Day 24: Marks, Kevin (2012). *Stations of the Cross* [Installation]. Mountain View, CA: The Highway Community.

Day 25: Lewis, C.S. *Letters to Malcom: Chiefly on Prayer.* Mariner Books, 2012.

Merton, Thomas. *The Seven Storey Mountain.* Mariner Books, 1999.

Day 26: Waltke, Bruce. *Finding the Will of God: A Pagan Notion?* Eerdmans, 2002.

Day 27: Wright, N.T. *Into God's Presence: Prayer in the New Testament.* Eerdmans, 2001.

Brown, Stuart. *Play: How It Shapes the Brain, Opens the Imagination, and Invigorates the Soul.* Avery, 2010.

Day 28: Crabb, Larry. *Becoming a True Spiritual Community: A Profound Vision of What the Church Can Be.* Thomas Nelson, 2007.

Day 29: Buechner, Frederick. *Listening to Your Life: Daily Meditations.* HarperOne, 1992.

Day 30: Phillips, Susan. *The Cultivated Life: From Ceaseless Striving to Receiving Joy.* IVP Books, 2015.

Day 31: Elliot, Elisabeth. *Secure in the Everlasting Arms.* Revell, 2004.

———. *Keep a Quiet Heart*. Revell, 2004.

Day 32: Terkeurst, Lysa. Proverbs 31 Ministries Facebook page. https://www.facebook.com/Prov31Ministries/photos/a.390955286960 .162138.99550061960/10153020716576961/?type=3&theater.

Day 33: Lessin, Roy. *Today Is Your Best Day*. New Leaf Press, 2012.

Day 34: Smith, Hannah Whitall. *The Christian's Secret of a Happy Life*. Revell, 2012.

Day 35: Manning, Brennan. *Souvenirs of Solitude: Finding Rest in Abba's Embrace*. NavPress, 2009.

Day 36: Willard, Dallas. *Divine Conspiracy: Rediscovering Our Hidden Life with God*. Harper, 1998.

Spiritual Gifts that are listed in the Bible include: prophecy, serving, teaching, encouragement, giving, leadership, mercy, prophet, evangelist, pastor, teacher, wisdom, knowledge, faith, healing, miracles, discernment, tongues, apostle, prophet, help, administration and service (Romans 12:6–8, 1 Corinthians 12: 8–10, 28, Ephesians 4:11, and 1 Peter 4:11).

Day 37: O'Connor, Flannery. *A Prayer Journal*. Farrar, Straus and Giroux, 2013.

Day 38: Peterson, Eugene. *Christ Plays in Ten Thousand Places*. Eerdmans, 2008.

Day 40: Merton, Thomas. *Thoughts in Solitude*. Farrar, Straus and Giroux, 1999.

Bonhoeffer, Dietrich. *Psalms: The Prayer Book of the Bible*. Augsberg Fortress, 1974.

Nouwen, Henri. *Turn My Mourning into Dancing*. Thomas Nelson. 2004.

Bibliography

Articles used in quoting studies for "Today's Beloved Challenge" sections

Day 1: Parker-Pope, Tara. "Writing Your Way to Happiness," *New York Times*, January 19, 2015. http://well.blogs.nytimes.com/2015/01/19/writing -your-way-to-happiness/?_r=0.

Day 2: Lewis, Tanya. "Scientists Discovered the Easiest Way to Boost Your Mood," *Business Insider*, June 29, 2015. http://www.businessinsider .com/walking-in-nature-boosts-your-mood-2015-6.

Day 3: Alban, Deane. "The Mental Health Benefits of Art Are for Everyone," Be Brain Fit, March 16, 2016. http://bebrainfit.com/the-health-benefits -of-art-are-for-everyone/.

Day 4: Telpner, Meghan. "The Surprising Health Benefits of Writing Love Letters (According to Science)," Mind Body Green, February 2, 2016. http://www.mindbodygreen.com/0-23540/the-surprising-health -benefits-of-writing-love-letters-according-to-science.html.

Day 6: Petersen, Neil. "4 Benefits of Self-Affirmation," All Psych, May 18, 2016. http://blog.allpsych.com/4-benefits-of-self-affirmation/.

Marche, Stephen. "Is Facebook Making Us Lonely?" *Atlantic*, May 2012. http://www.theatlantic.com/magazine/archive/2012/05/is-face book-making-us-lonely/308930/.

Day 7: Alleyne, Richard. "A Cup of Tea Really Can Help Reduce Stress in Times of Crisis, Claim Scientists," *Telegraph*, August 13, 2009. http://www.telegraph.co.uk/news/science/science-news/6015821/ A-cup-of-tea-really-can-help-reduce-stress-at-times-of-crisis-claim -scientists.html.

Dwyer, Marge. "Coffee Drinking Tied to Lower Risk of Suicide," *Harvard Gazette*, July 24, 2013. http://news.harvard.edu/gazette/story/2013/07/drinking-coffee-may-reduce-risk-of-suicide-by-50/.

Jacques, Renee. "11 Reasons You Should Drink Coffee Every Day," *Huffington Post*, November 9, 2015. http://www.huffingtonpost.com/2013/10/17/coffee-health-benefits_n_4102133.html.

Day 8: Seppala, Emma M. "The Science Behind the Joy of Sharing Joy," *Psychology Today*, July 15, 2013. https://www.psychologytoday.com/blog/feeling-it/201307/the-science-behind-the-joy-sharing-joy.

Day 10: Clores, Suzanne. "The Benefits of Quiet for Body, Mind and Spirit," *Next Avenue*, February 9, 2012. http://www.nextavenue.org/benefits-quiet-body-mind-and-spirit/.

Day 11: Shaw, Gina. "Water and Stress Reduction: Sipping Stress Away." *WebMD*, July 7, 2009. http://www.webmd.com/diet/features/water-stress-reduction.

Mann, Denise. "Even Mild Dehydration May Cause Emotional, Physical Problems," *WebMD*, January 20, 2012. http://www.webmd.com/women/news/20120120/even-mild-dehydration-may-cause-emotional-physical-problems#1.

Day 12: Thorpe, J. R. "6 Health Benefits of Taking Baths," *Bustle*, November 18, 2015. http://www.bustle.com/articles/124641-6-health-benefits-of-taking-baths.

Day 13: http://www.aboutflowers.com/health-benefits-a-research/emotional-impact-of-flowers-study.html.

http://www.aboutflowers.com/health-benefits-a-research/flowers-a-morning-moods-study.html.

Day 14: Wilson, Jacque. "This Is Your Brain on Crafting," *CNN*, January 5, 2015. http://www.cnn.com/2014/03/25/health/brain-crafting-benefits/.

Day 15: "2 Minutes to a Happier You," *Prevention*, February 3, 2015. http://www.prevention.com/mind-body/instant-mood-boosting-tricks.

Day 16: Babauta, Leo. "5 Powerful Reasons to Eat Slower," *Zen Habits*, July 13, 2007. http://zenhabits.net/5-powerful-reasons-to-eat-slower/.

Day 17: Colino, Stacey. "The Health Benefits of Hugging," *U.S. News & World Report*, February 3, 2016. http://health.usnews.com/health-news/health-wellness/articles/2016-02-03/the-health-benefits-of-hugging.

Day 18: Mehta, Vinita. "How to Use All 5 Senses to Beat Stress," *Psychology Today*, February 4, 2015. https://www.psychologytoday.com/blog/head-games/201502/how-use-all-5-senses-beat-stress.

Day 19: "Vitamin C: Stress Buster," *Psychology Today*, April 25, 2003. https://www.psychologytoday.com/articles/200304/vitamin-c-stress-buster.

Day 20: Hrala, Josh. "Looking at Trees Can Reduce Your Stress Levels, Even in the Middle of a City," Science Alert, May 8, 2016. http://www.science alert.com/urban-tree-coverage-can-significantly-reduce-stress-study -finds.

Boult, Adam. "Being Around Trees Makes You Less Stressed—Study," *Telegraph*, May 6, 2016. http://www.telegraph.co.uk/science/2016/05/06/being-around-trees-makes-you-less-stressed—study/.

Day 21: Santos, Elena. "Coloring Isn't Just for Kids. It Can Actually Help Adults Combat Stress," *Huffington Post*, October 13, 2014. http://www.huffingtonpost.com/2014/10/13/coloring-for-stress_n_5975832.html.

Day 22: Drummond, Katie. "The Best Essential Oil for Stress?" *Prevention*, August 8, 2012. http://www.prevention.com/mind-body/emotional -health/scent-citrus-shown-reduce-stress.

Holmes, Lindsay. "11 Scents That Can Do Wonders for Your Well-Being," *Huffington Post*, April 26, 2014. http://www.huffingtonpost.com/2014/04/26/scents-and-wellbeing_n_5193609.html.

Day 23: Wolpert, Stuart. "Putting Feelings into Words Produces Therapeutic Effects in the Brain; UCLA Neuroimaging Study Supports Ancient Buddhist Teachings," UCLA Newsroom, June 21, 2007. http://news room.ucla.edu/releases/Putting-Feelings-Into-Words-Produces-8047.

Day 24: Preidt, Robert. "What a 30-Minute Nap Can Do for Your Health," CBS News, February 11, 2015. http://www.cbsnews.com/news/what-a-30-minute-nap-can-do-for-your-health/.

"Assess Your Sleep Needs," Healthy Sleep, Division of Sleep Medicine, Harvard Medical School. http://healthysleep.med.harvard.edu/need -sleep/what-can-you-do/assess-needs.

Day 25: Neuman, Brooke. "10 Shocking Benefits of Listening to Classical Music," Take Lessons, January 22, 2016. http://takelessons.com/blog/benefits-of-listening-to-classical-music-z15.

Day 26: Cooper, Belle Beth. "10 Simple Ways Science Backed Ways to Be Happier Today," Good Think, August 12, 2013. http://goodthinkinc .com/project/fast-company-10-simple-science-backed-ways-to-be -happier-today/.

Lickerman, Alex. "Leveraging Anticipatory Joy," *Psychology Today*, January 13, 2013. https://www.psychologytoday.com/blog/happiness-in-world/201301/leveraging-anticipatory-joy.

Day 27: Brown, Stuart. *Stuart Brown: Play Is More Than Just Fun*, TED, video file, May 2008. http://www.ted.com/talks/stuart_brown_says_play_is _more_than_fun_it_s_vital.

Day 28: Hamby, Sherry. "Resilience and...4 Benefits to Sharing Your Story," *Psychology Today*, September 3, 2013. https://www.psychology today.com/blog/the-web-violence/201309/resilience-and-4-benefits -sharing-your-story.

"Friendships: Enrich Your Life and Improve Your Health," Mayo Clinic. http://www.mayoclinic.org/healthy-lifestyle/adult-health/in-depth/ friendships/art-20044860.

Day 30: Scutti, Susan. "Nature Sounds, Independent of the Beautiful Scenery, Helps Boost Your Mood," Medical Daily, October 10, 2014. http://www.medicaldaily.com/nature-sounds-independent-beautiful -scenery-helps-boost-your-mood-306745.

McGregor, Scott. "How to Increase Workflow and Reduce Stress with Nature Sounds," *Smashing Magazine*, October 29, 2015. https://www .smashingmagazine.com/2015/10/increase-workflow-reduce-stress -with-nature-sounds/.

Day 31: Fowler, Paige. "How Cleaning and Organizing Can Improve Your Physical and Mental Health," *Shape*, January 29, 2015. http://www .shape.com/lifestyle/mind-and-body/how-cleaning-and-organizing -can-improve-your-physical-and-mental-health.

Day 32: Muther, Christopher. "What Is the Color of Hope?" Boston.com, March 19, 2009. http://archive.boston.com/lifestyle/house/articles/ 2009/03/19/what_is_the_color_of_hope/?page=2.

Day 33: Groth, Aimee. "If You Want to Be Happy, Stop Comparing Yourself to Others," *Business Insider*, April 21, 2013. http://www.business insider.com/happiness-research-2013-4.

Grant, Megan. "4 Science-Backed Reasons to Take a Break from Social Media," Bustle.com. https://www.bustle.com/articles/149890-4-science -backed-reasons-to-take-a-break-from-social-media.

Day 34: William, David K. "10 Amazing Health Benefits of Sun Exposure," Lifehack. http://www.lifehack.org/articles/lifestyle/10-amazing -health-benefits-sun-exposure.html.

Day 35: Parker-Pope, Tara. "Reinventing Date Night for Long-Married Couples," *New York Times*, February 12, 2008. http://www.nytimes .com/2008/02/12/health/12well.html?_r=0.

Day 36: Whalen, Jeanne. "A Road to Mental Health Through the

Kitchen," *Wall Street Journal*, December 8, 2014. http://www.wsj.com/articles/a-road-to-mental-health-through-the-kitchen-1418059204.

Day 37: Alban, Deane. "The Mental Health Benefits of Art Are for Everyone," Be Brain Fit, March 16, 2016. http://bebrainfit.com/the-health-benefits-of-art-are-for-everyone/.

Day 38: Wise, Abigail. "8 Science-Backed Reasons to Read a (Real) Book," RealSimple.com. http://www.realsimple.com/health/preventative-health/benefits-of-reading-real-books.

Bushak, Lecia. "E-books Are Damaging Your Health: Why We should All Start Reading Paper Books Again," Medical Daily, 1/11/15. http://www.medicaldaily.com/e-books-are-damaging-your-health-why-we-should-all-start-reading-paper-books-again-317212.

Day 40: Kamen, Randy. "The Transformative Power of Gratitude," *Huffington Post*, April 1, 2015. http://www.huffingtonpost.com/randy-kamen-gredinger/the-transformative-power-_2_b_6982152.html.

Articles used in researching content in "Today's Beloved Challenges," but not quoted as a study

Day 5: Ulbrecht, Catherine. "Music Therapy for Health and Wellness," *Psychology Today*, June 21, 2013. https://www.psychologytoday.com/blog/natural-standard/201306/music-therapy-health-and-wellness.

Day 15: Korb, Alex. "Boosting Your Seratonin Activity," *Psychology Today*, November 17, 2011. https://www.psychologytoday.com/blog/prefrontal-nudity/201111/boosting-your-serotonin-activity.

Day 19: Glassman, Keri. "13 Foods That Fight Stress," *Prevention*, May 22, 2014. http://www.prevention.com/mind-body/emotional-health/13-healthy-foods-that-reduce-stress-and-depression/slide/7.

"All About the Fruit Group," USDA, July 16, 2016. https://www.chosemyplate.ov/fruit.

Day 27: "The Benefits of Play for Adults," HelpGuide.org http://www.helpguide.org/articles/emotional-health/benefits-of-play-for-adults.htm.

Tartakovsky, Margarita. "The Importance of Play for Adults," PsychCentral, November 15, 2012. http://psychcentral.com/blog/archives/2012/11/15/the-importance-of-play-for-adults/.

Day 29: Different Tea Benefits

black tea: http://www.webmd.com/food-recipes/20061005/drinking-black-tea-may-soothe-stress.

green tea: http://springarborliving.com/senior-assisted-living-blog/green
_tea_can_help_reduce_anxiety_stress_and_depression_in_elderly.

chamomile tea: http://www.naturalhealth365.com/chamomile.html/.

peppermint tea: http://www.telegraph.co.uk/food-and-drink/news/from
-peppermint-to-oolong-the-health-benefits-of-different-teas/.

Day 32: "Colors Psychology: The Emotional Effects of Colors," Art Therapy
Blog. http://www.arttherapyblog.com/online/color-psychology-psycho
logica-effects-of-colors/#.WBoi2pMrJ0J.

"Colors And Mood: How Colors You Wear Affect You," College Fashion,
May 5, 2009. http://www.collegefashion.net/fashion-tips/colors-and
-mood-how-the-colors-you-wear-affect-you/.

Day 39: Clair, Alicia Ann, "Music Therapy," Alzheimer's Foundation of America. http://www.alzfdn.org/EducationandCare/musictherapy.html.

Decker, Ed. "Music and Memory: Why Some Songs Mean So Much to Us,"
Rewire.com. https://www.rewireme.com/happiness/music-memory
-songs-mean-much-us/.

Articles used in researching content for types of prayers in "Prayer & Rest" sections

Day 2: Breath Prayers. https://gravitycenter.com/practice/breath-prayer/.

Day 12: Praying the Psalms. http://www.christianitytoday.com/ct/2008/
october/35.88.html.

Day 24: The Daily Examen. http://www.ignatianspirituality.com/ignatian
-prayer/the-examen#reflections.

Whispers of Rest

|| Connect with Bonnie!

Download
your FREE
Small Group Guide
& printables today!

Find resources and tools to help you
experience God's peace and presence
and spark joy with friends and deepen community.

* *Small Group Guide* | spark small group conversations
* *Pray-and-Rest Podcast* | audio guided quiet time
* *Weekly Journal Page* | journal your prayers
* *Be Beloved Coloring Pages* | color God's Word into your soul
* *Devotional Videos* | encourage your heart
  & more!

For your personal enrichment or meaningful group study.

Visit www.TheBonnieGray.com/whispersofrest
to download your free resources today!